Americarna

A Truck Driver's Photographic Odyssey

By Rodney Bishop

Foreward

*Looking at America as a whole, we see a land of immense
beauty and natural splendors. When one looks closer, we
begin to see the diversity of ways out land is being used and
preserved. That is exactly what Rodney Bishop has captured in his
travels across America. The life of a long haul trucker takes him to
places sometimes off the beaten path...away from the usual tourist
destinations...the real America! He began making photos of places he
found interesting along the way to deliver his loads. From speeding
along the Interstate to the red clay dirt roads of Alabama, his world
is one of the working man. With nothing more than his cell phone
camera, he has captured vignettes of America along the way.
Each photo in its own is simply a spot along the way.
Together, they paint a photographic essay of our country through
Rodney's eyes. He didn't set out to become a photographer or
documentarian of his travels. It was just his natural appreciation
of the places he gets to see each day from the elevated cab of his truck.
Thanks Rodney, for letting us ride along on your journey..*

Earl Carter

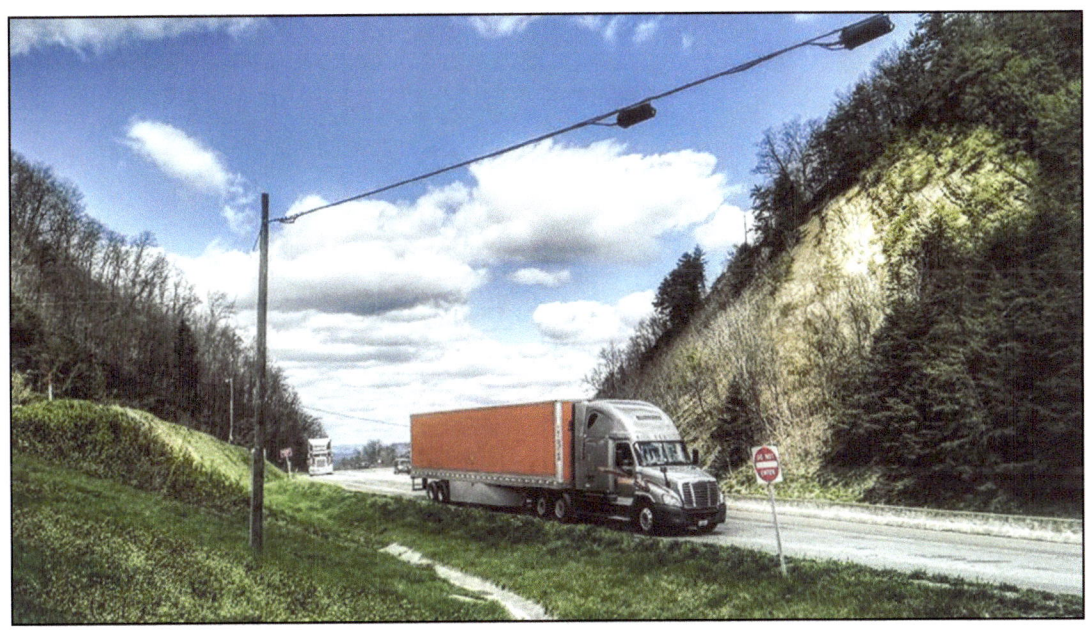

Rodney's Truck
Thorn Hill, Tennessee

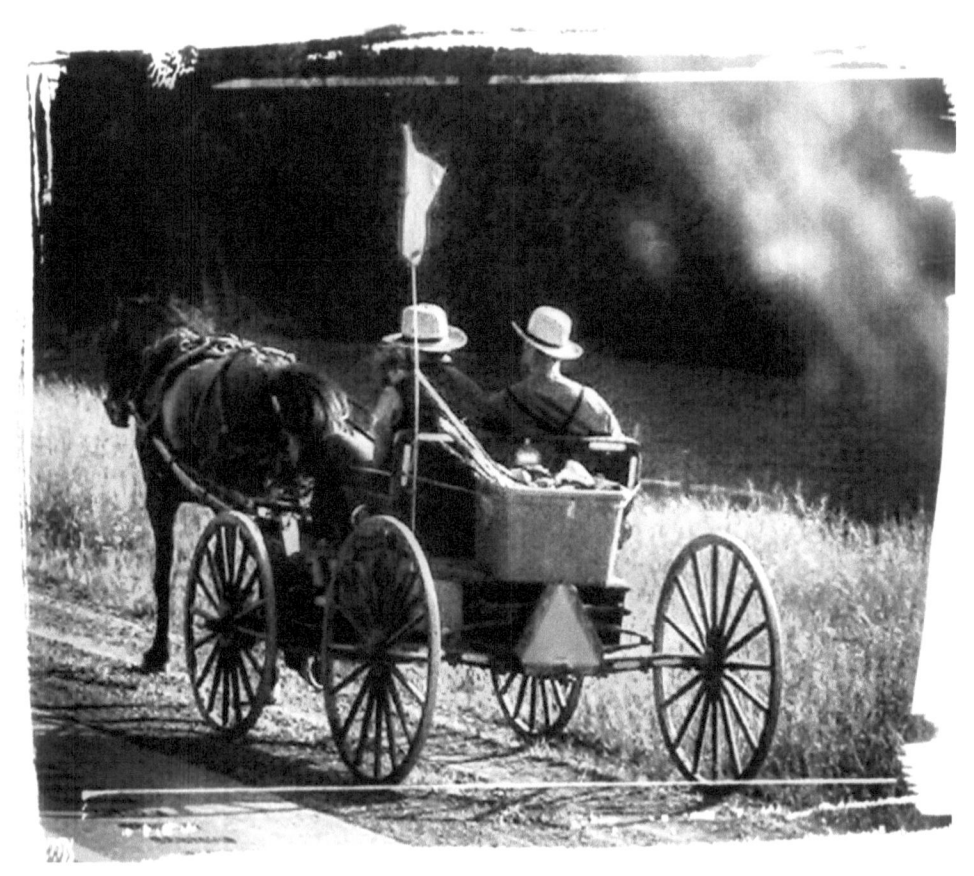

Amish Country, Middle Tennessee

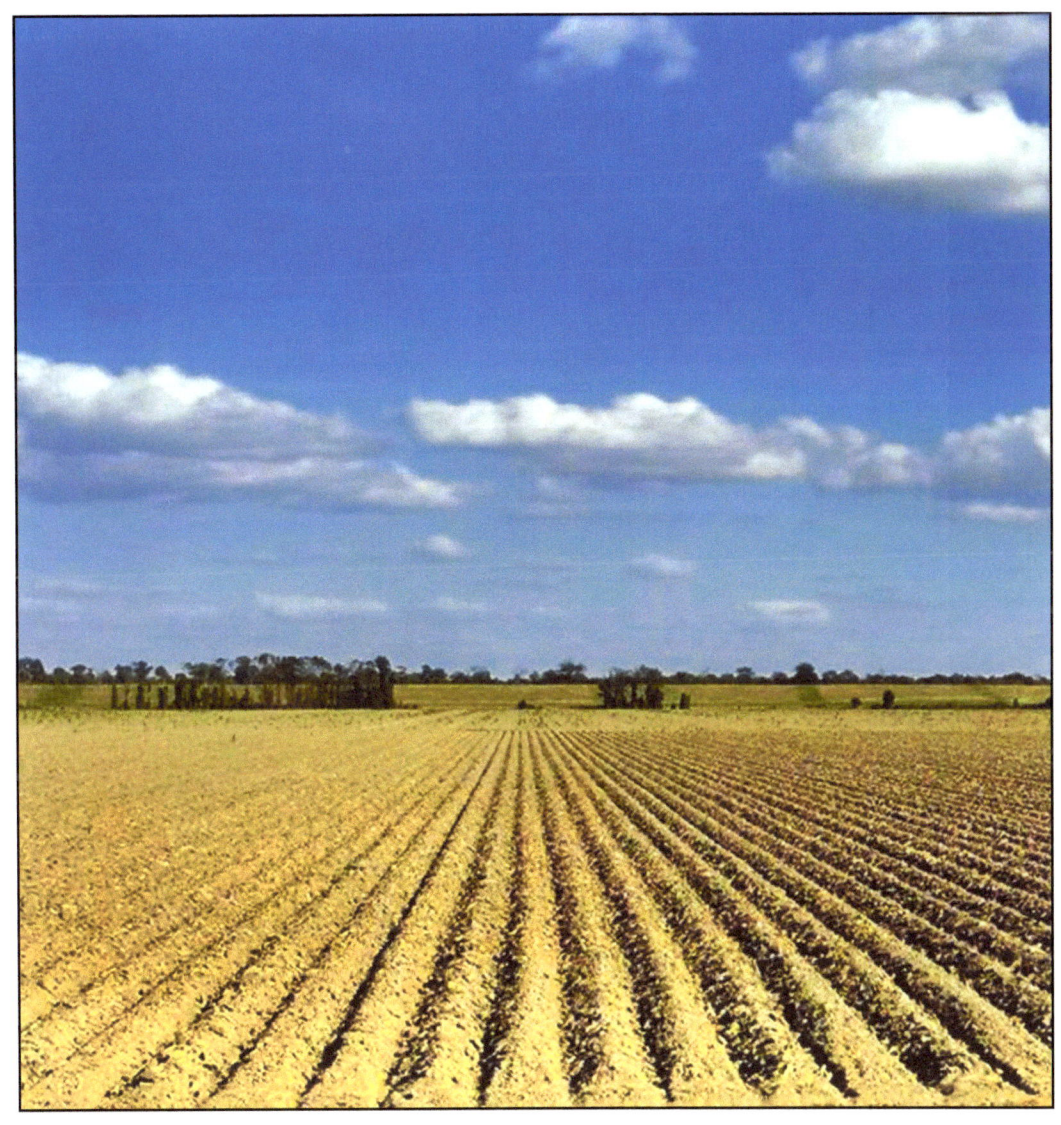

Louisiana

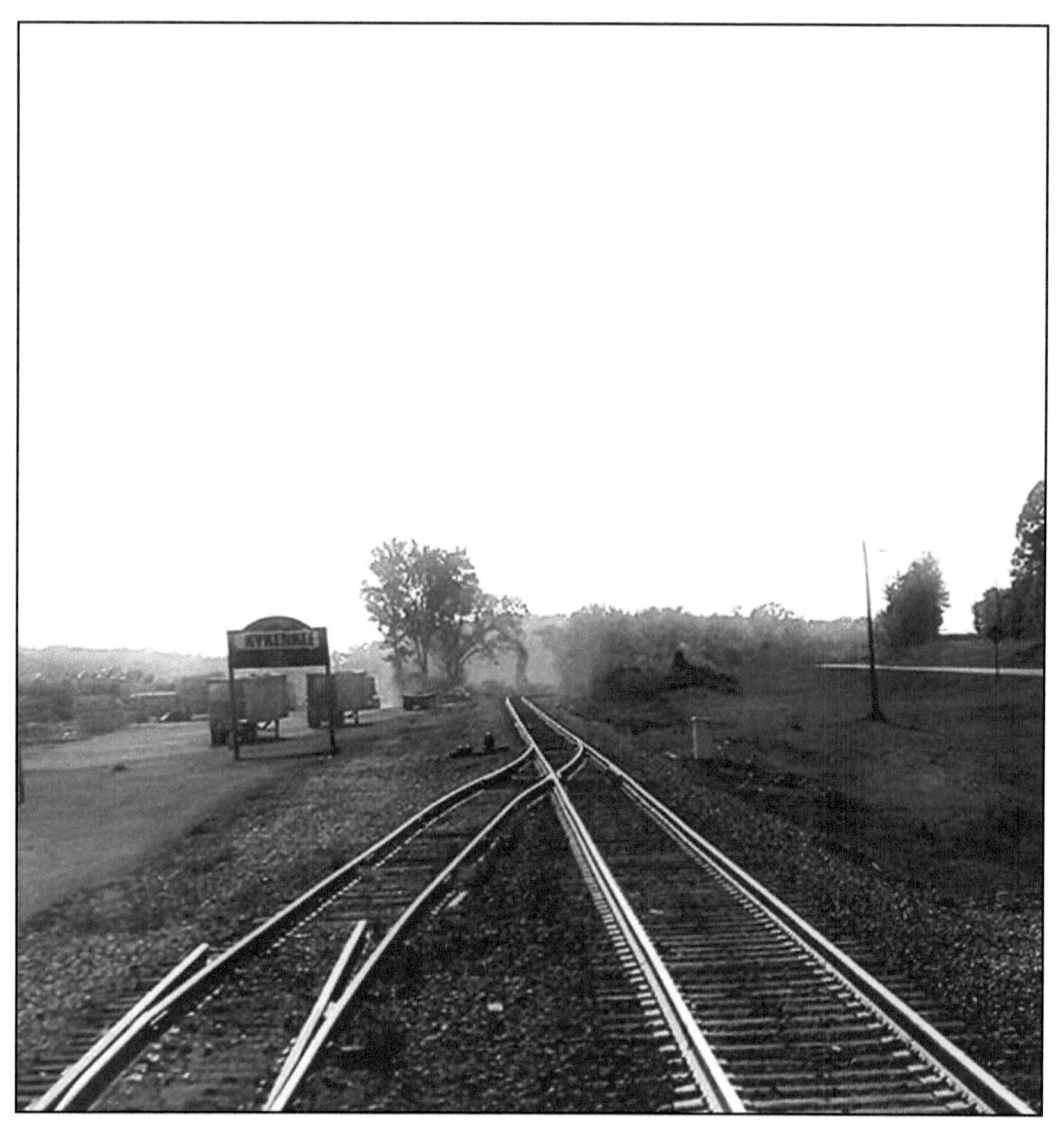

Solon, Ohio

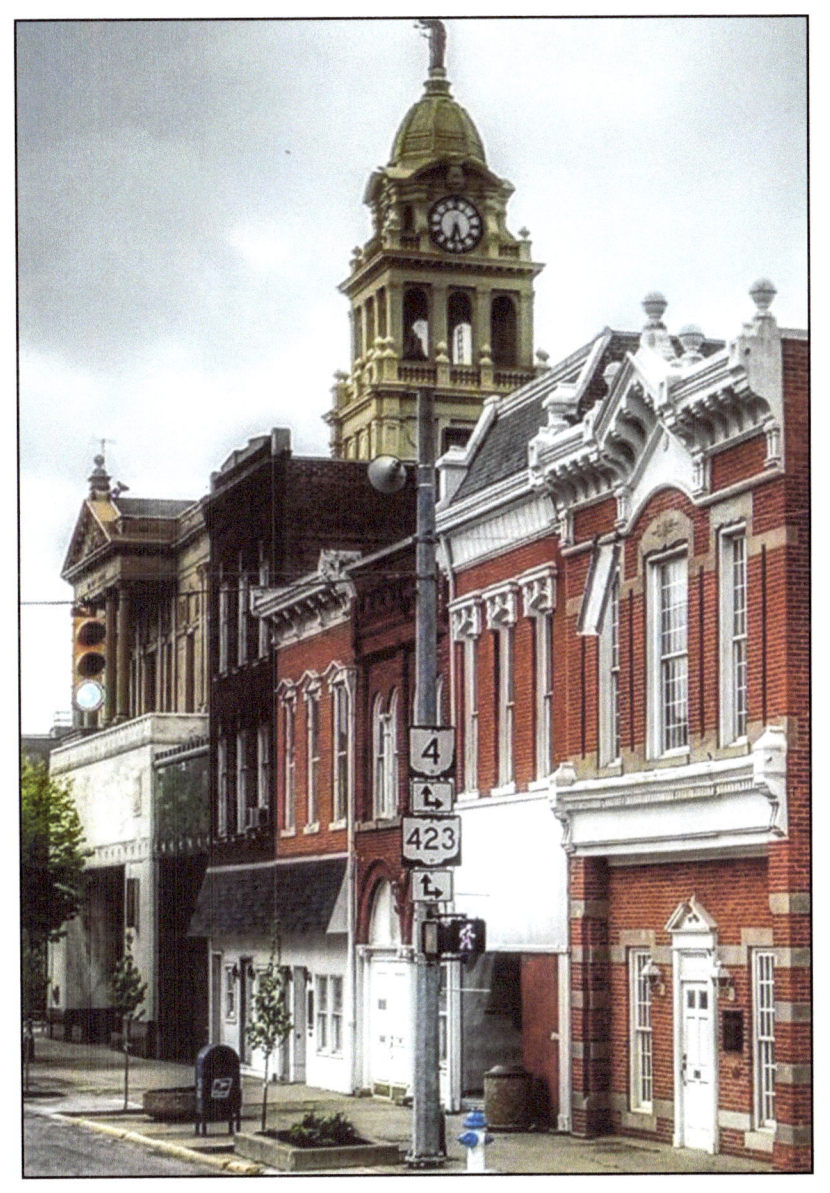

Marion, Ohio
The Marion County Courthouse towers over the historic downtown area.

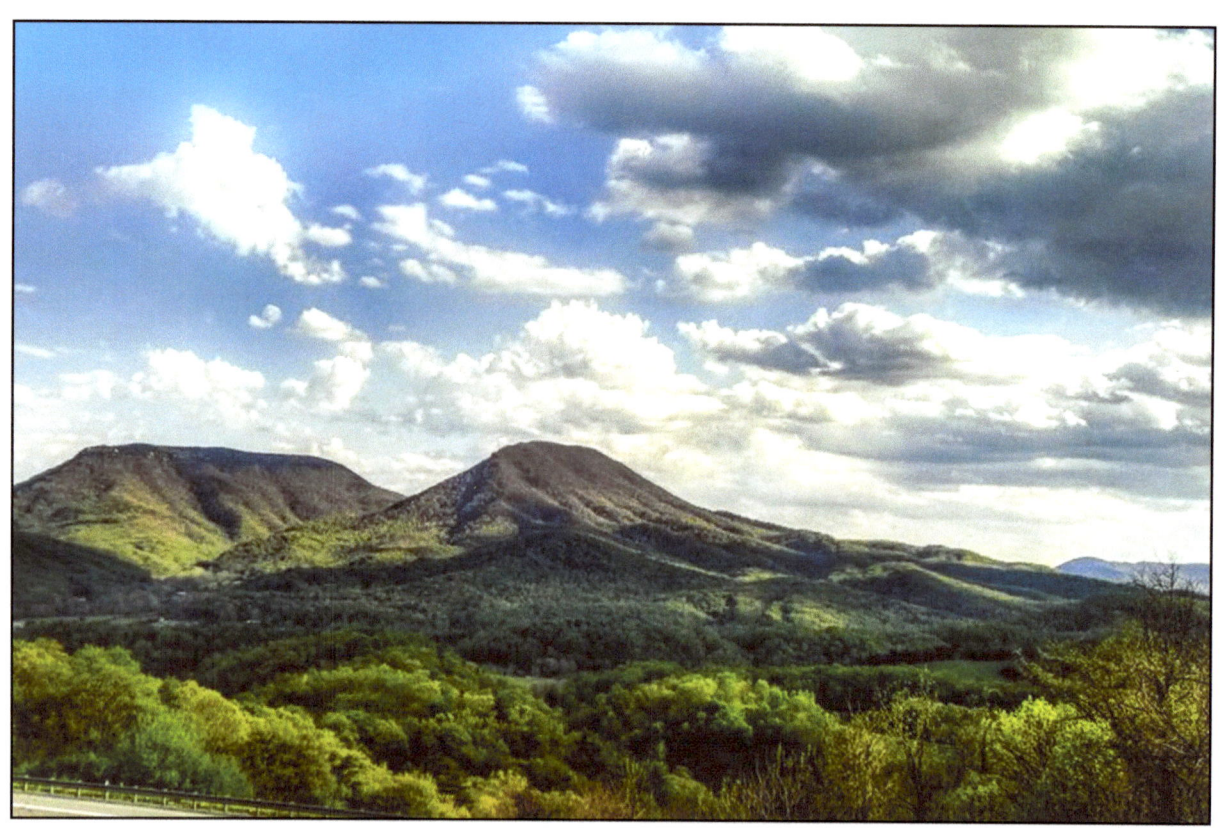

Twin Peaks, West Virginia/Virginia Line

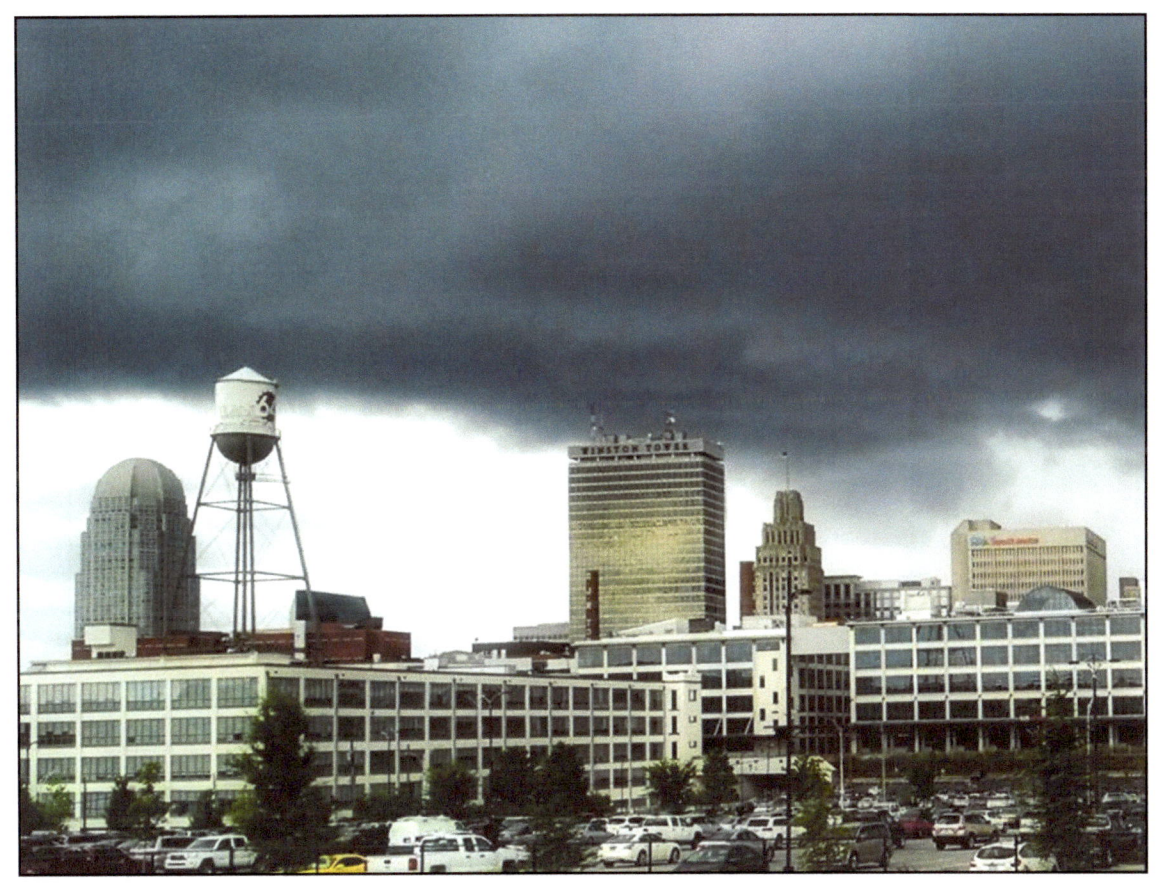

Winston-Salem, North Carolina
Winston Salem is a product of merging the two neighboring towns of Winston and Salem in 1913.
In 1875, R J Reynolds founded R. J. Reynolds Tobacco Company and the city became the
cigarette producing capital of the world.

Central Ohio
Amish and traditional farms are plentiful across the midwest.

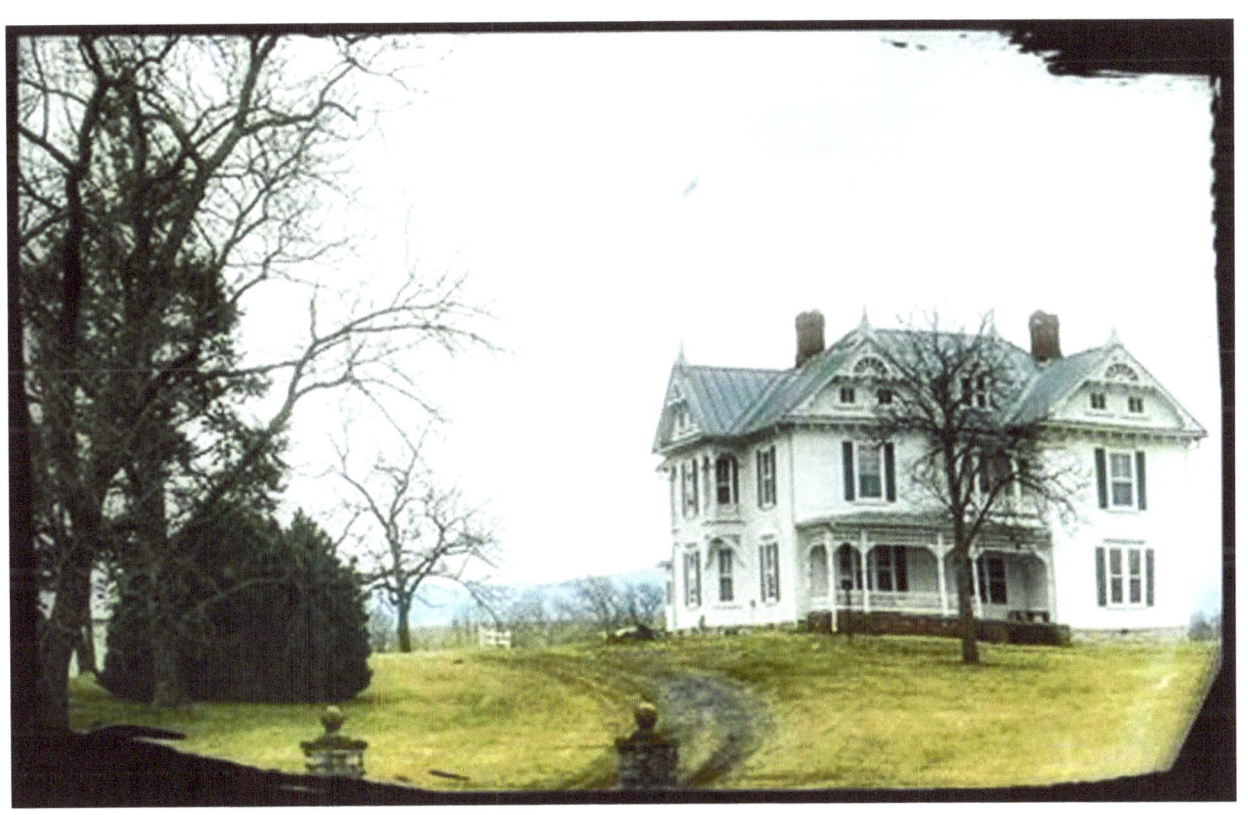

Waynesboro, Virginia

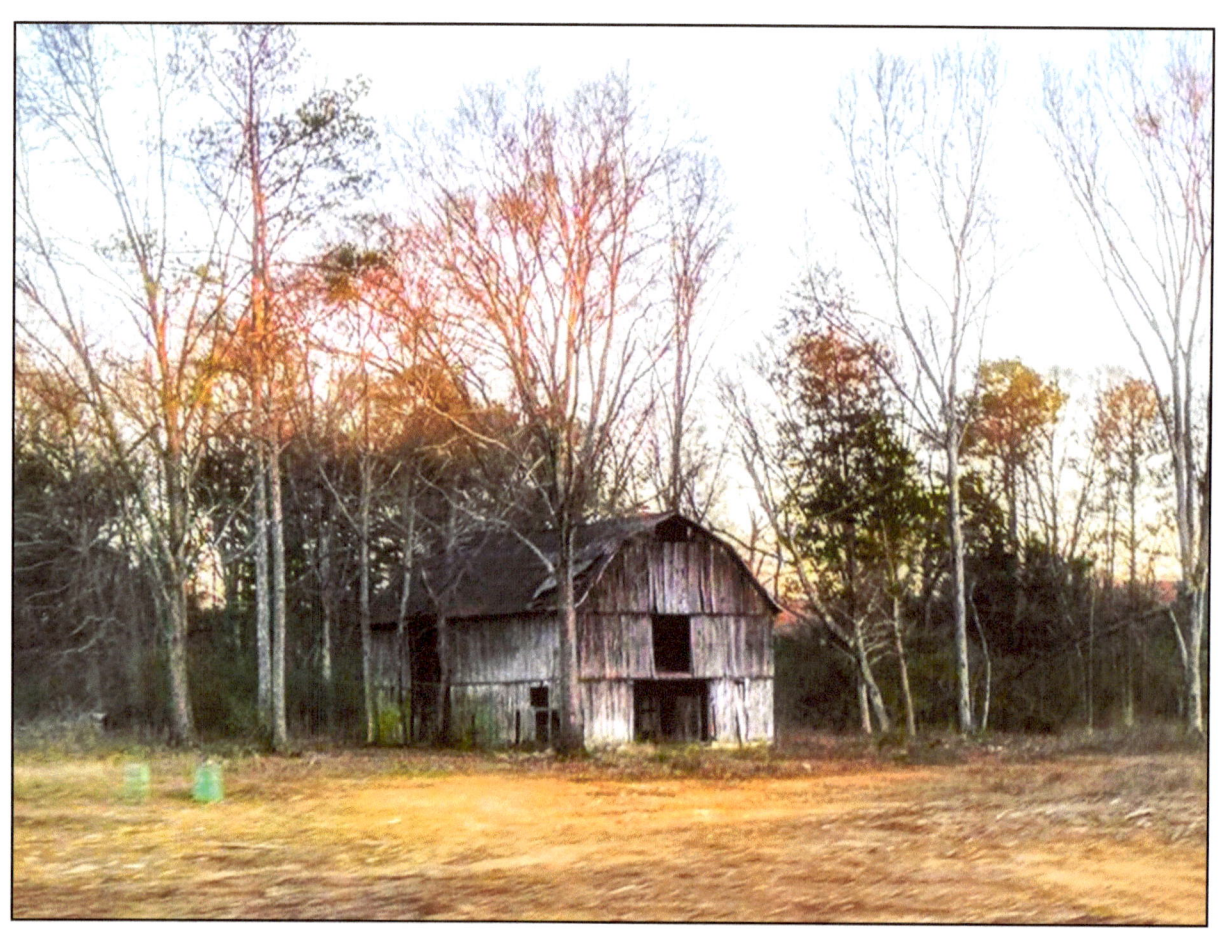

Near Lake Guntersville, Alabama

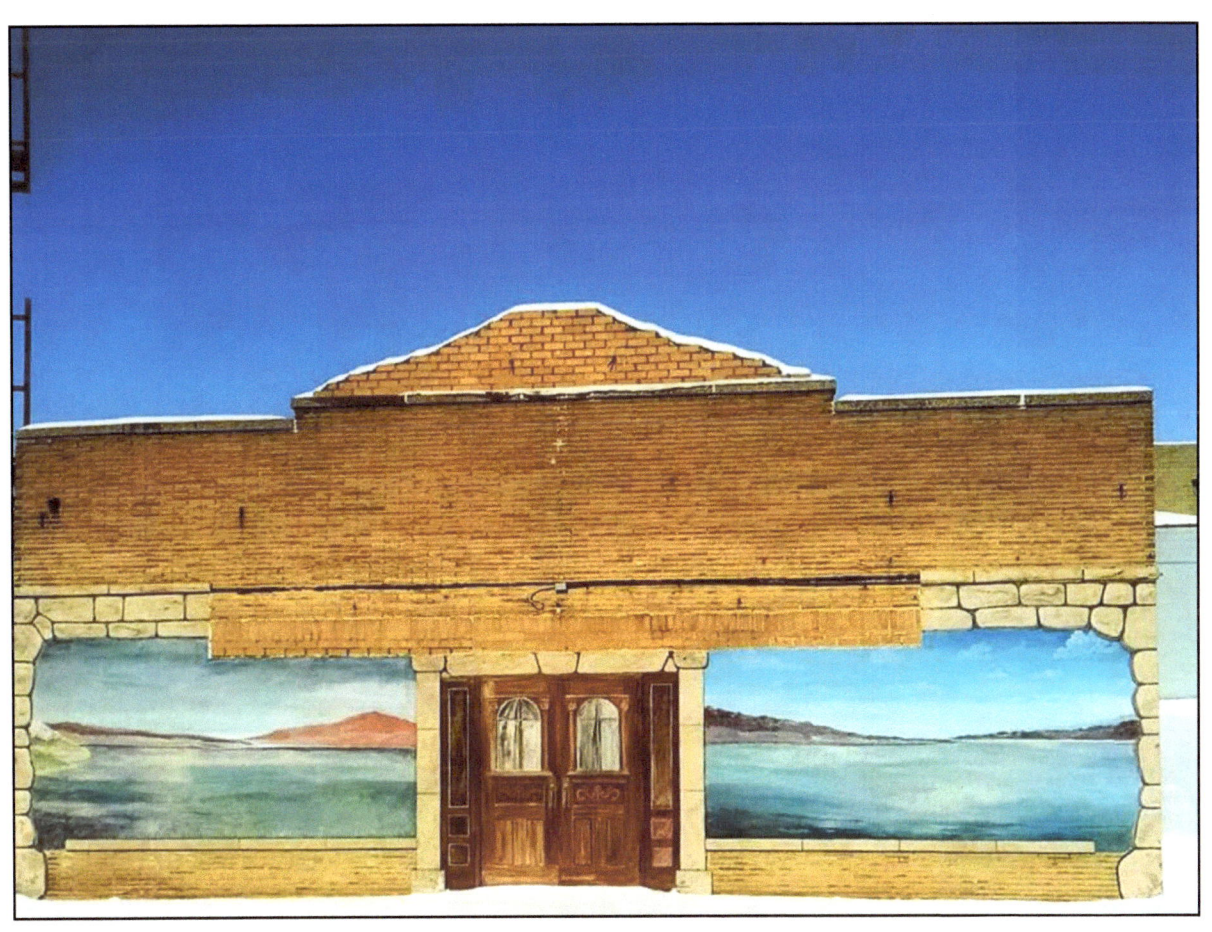

Jefferson, Indiana

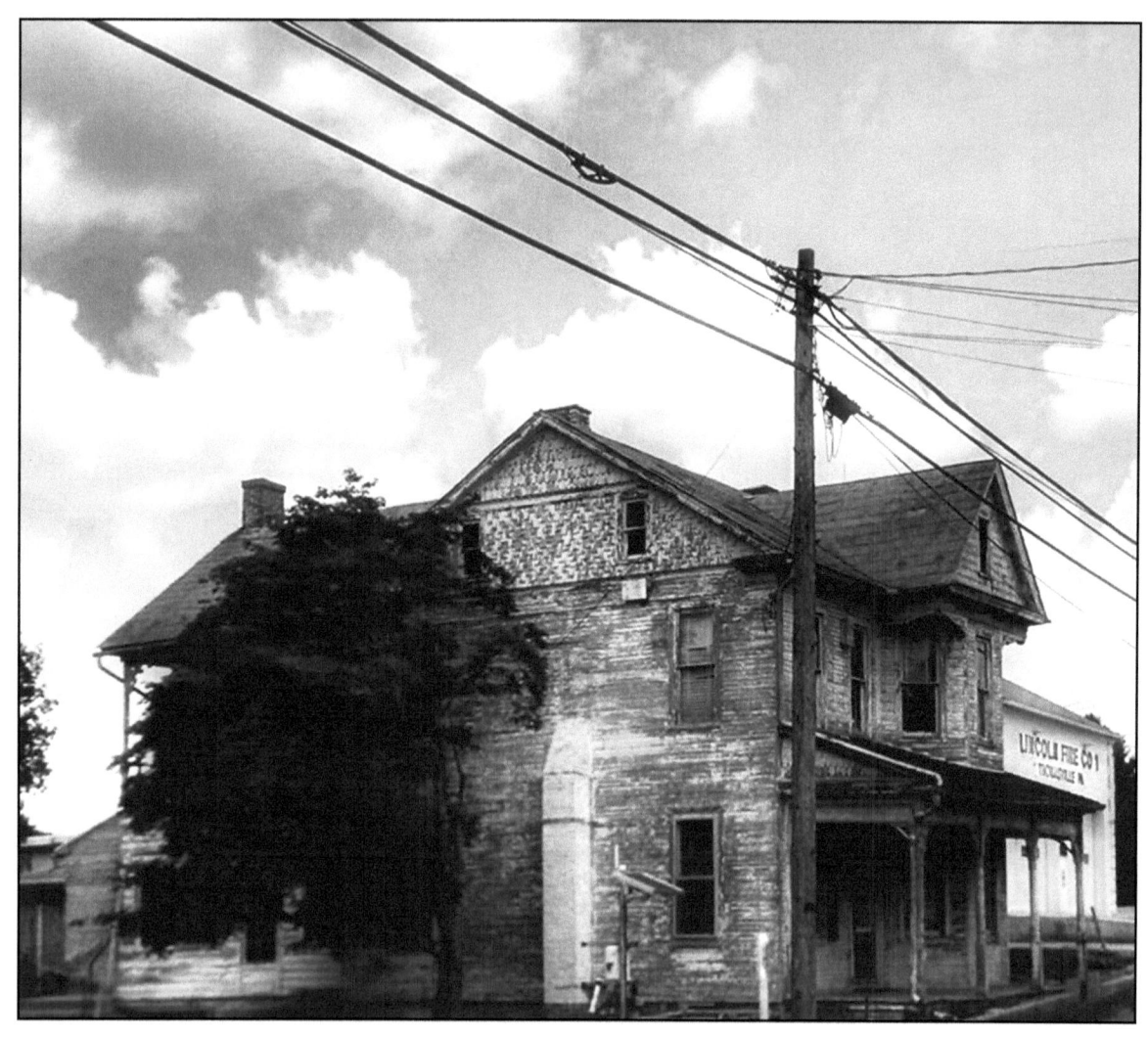

Thomasville, Pennsylvania

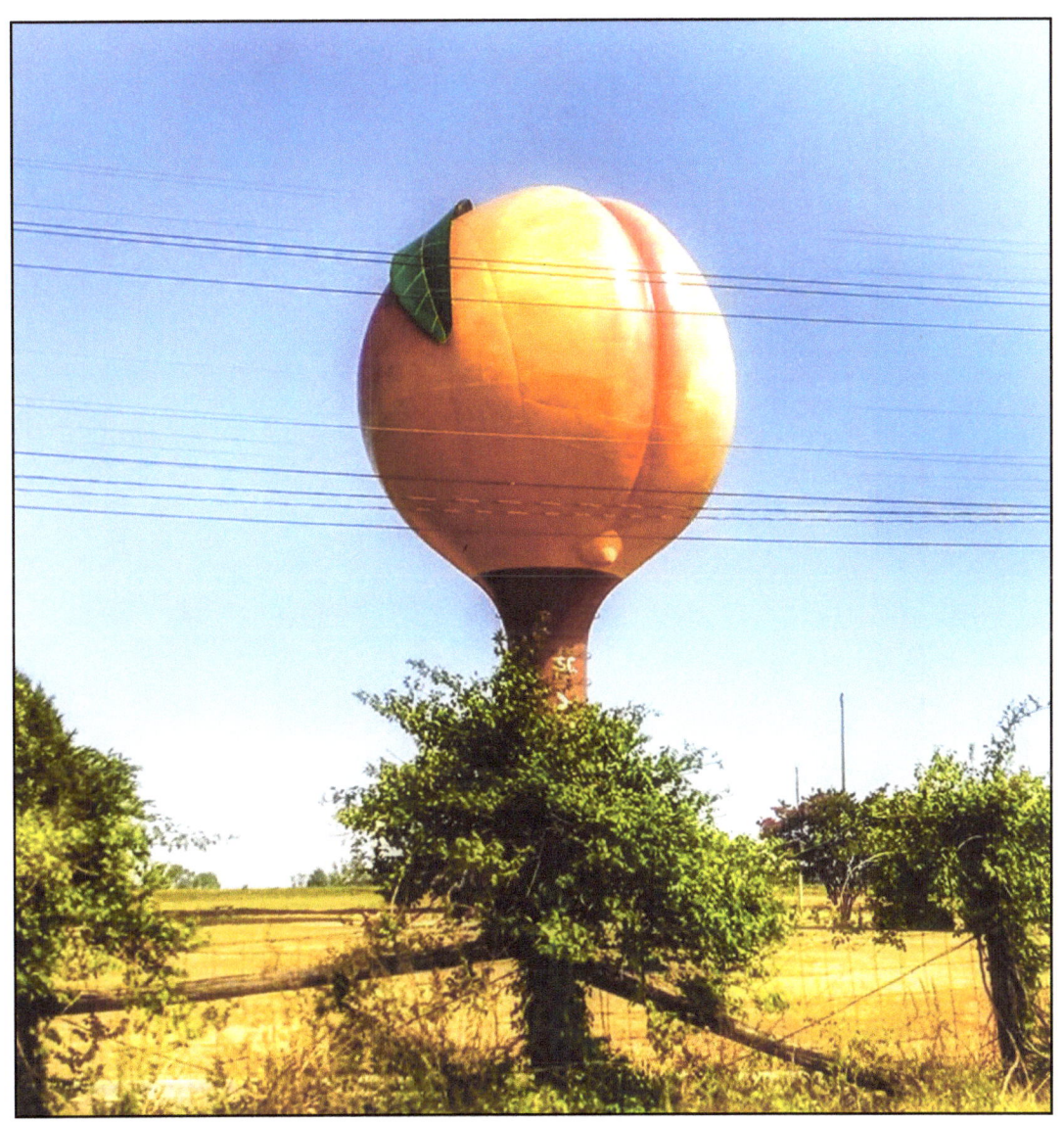

Gaffney, South Carolina
The Peachoid is a 135 feet tall water tower in Gaffney, South Carolina.
Upstate town's giant peach has a cameo appearance on Netflix drama 'House of Cards.'"

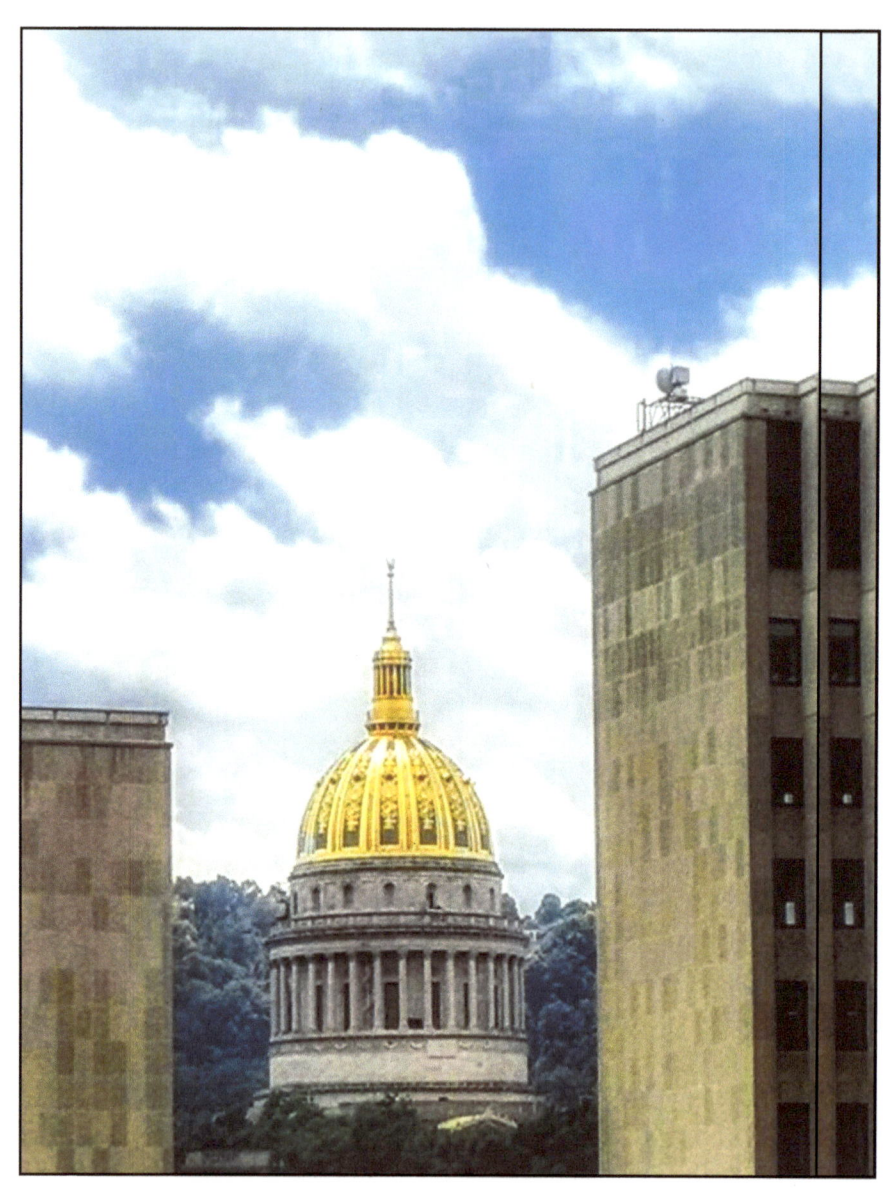

Charleston, West Virginia
The capitol dome is gilded with real gold.

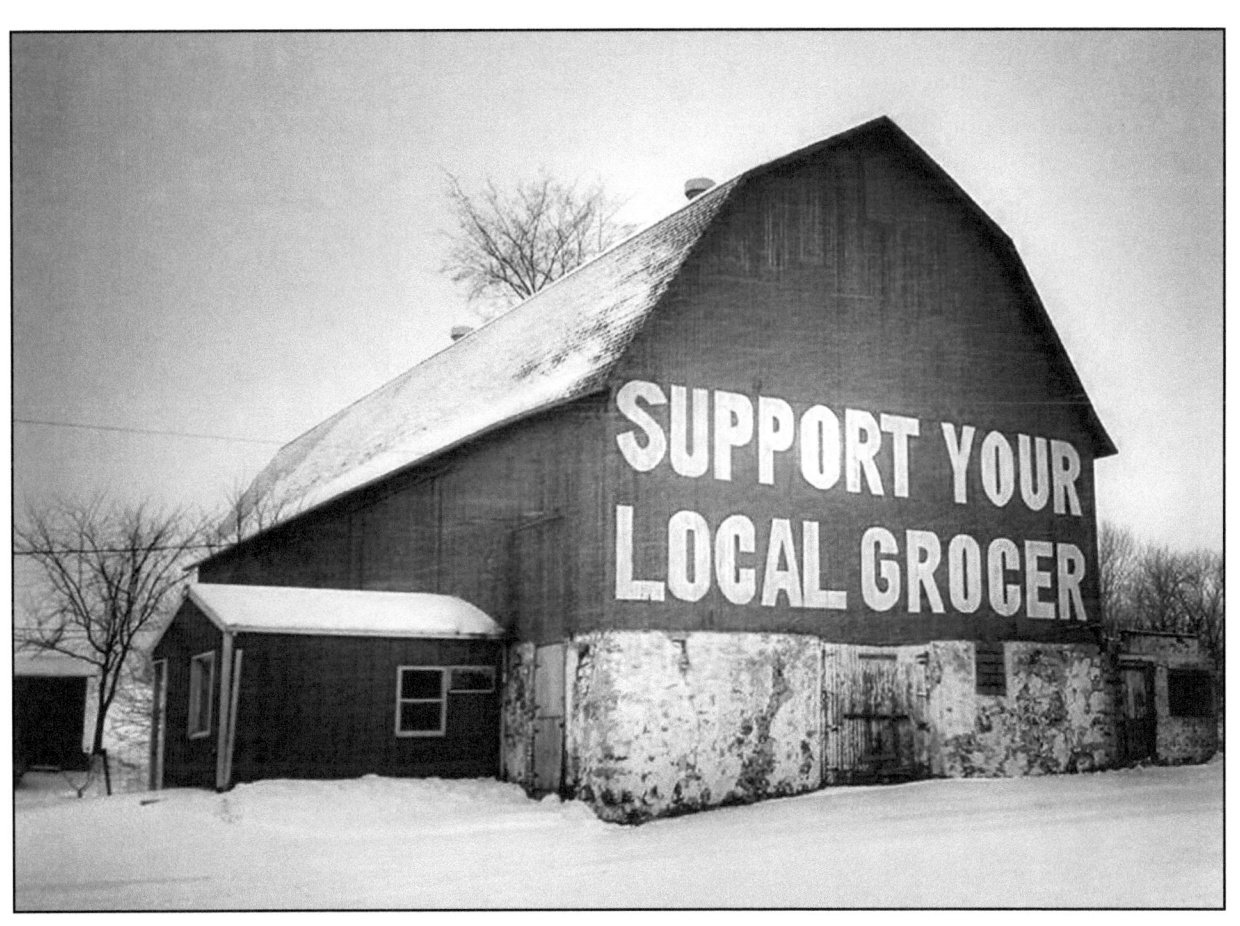

Iron Ridge, Wisconsin

Chattanooga, Tennessee

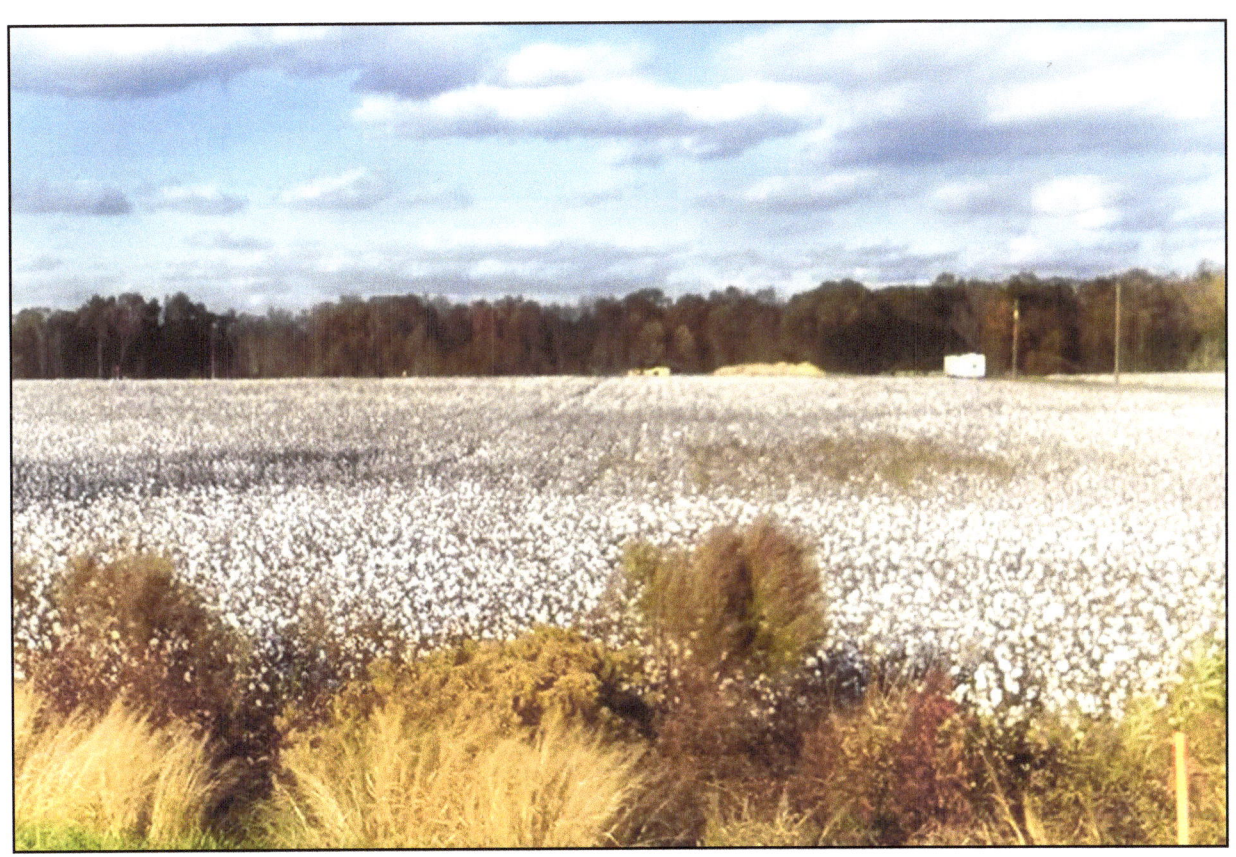

Eastern Virginia

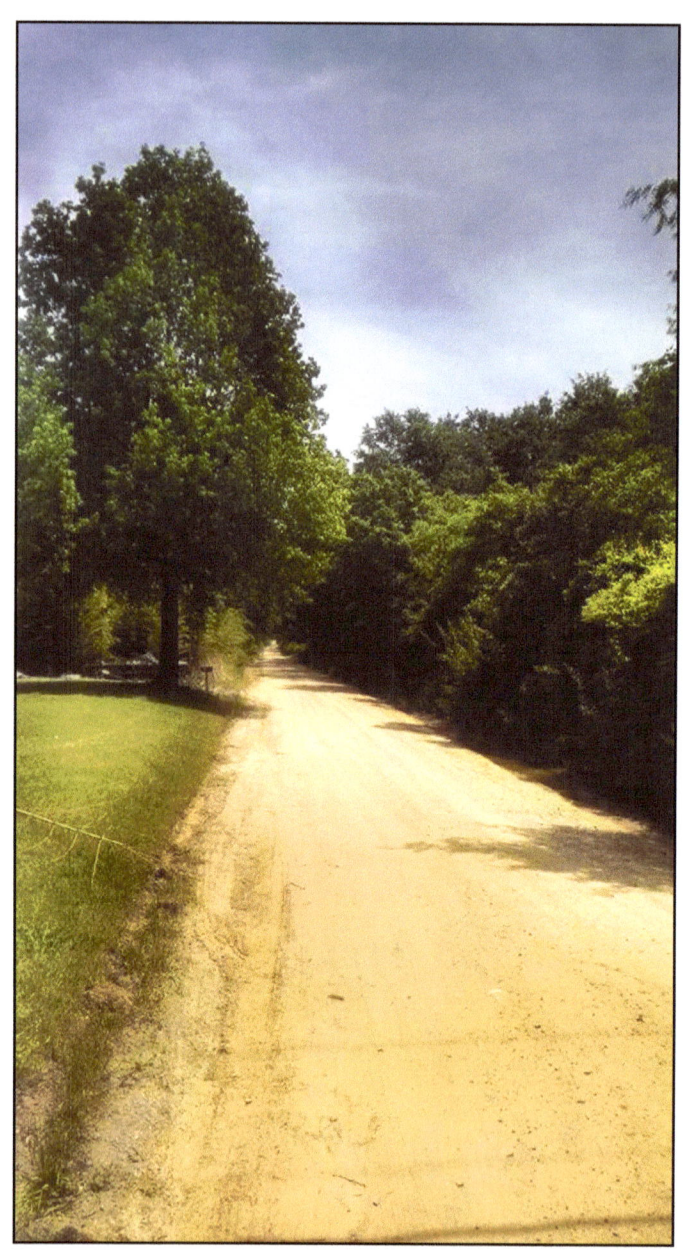

Lebanon, Tennessee

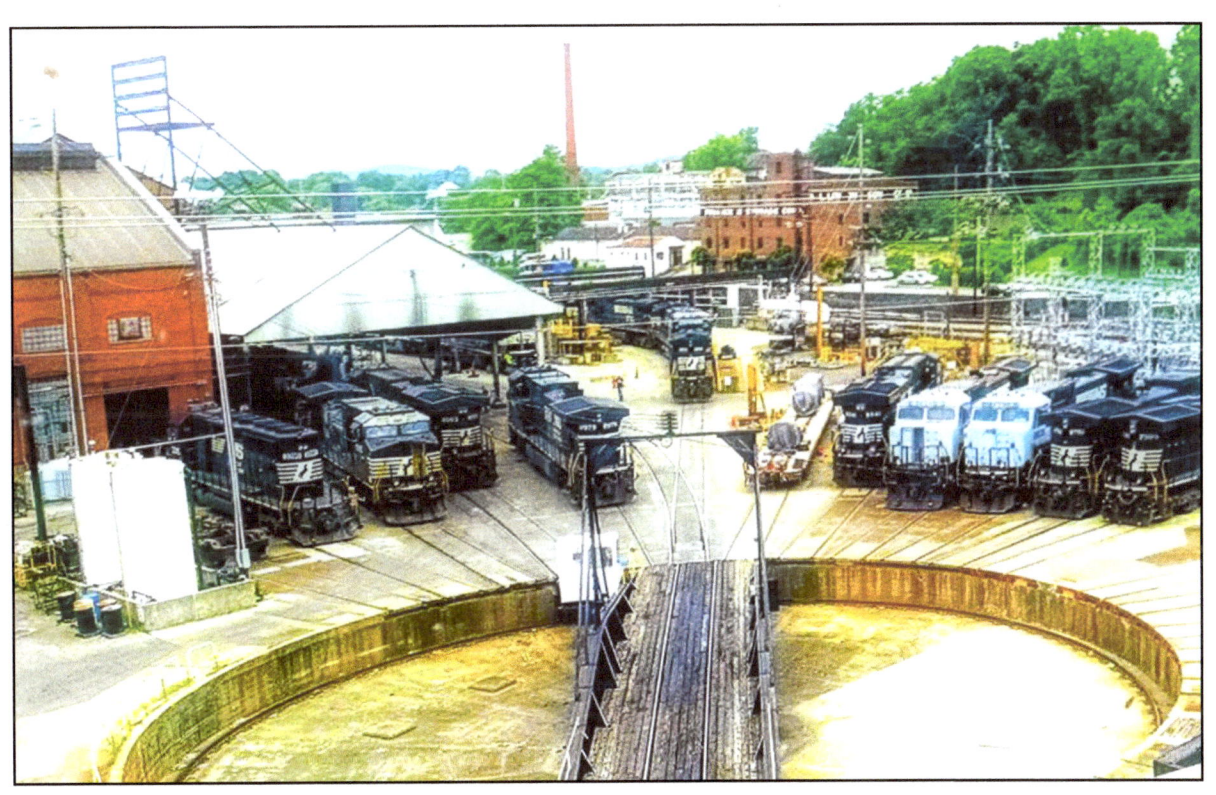

Roanoke, Virginia
Norfolk Southern locomotive shop

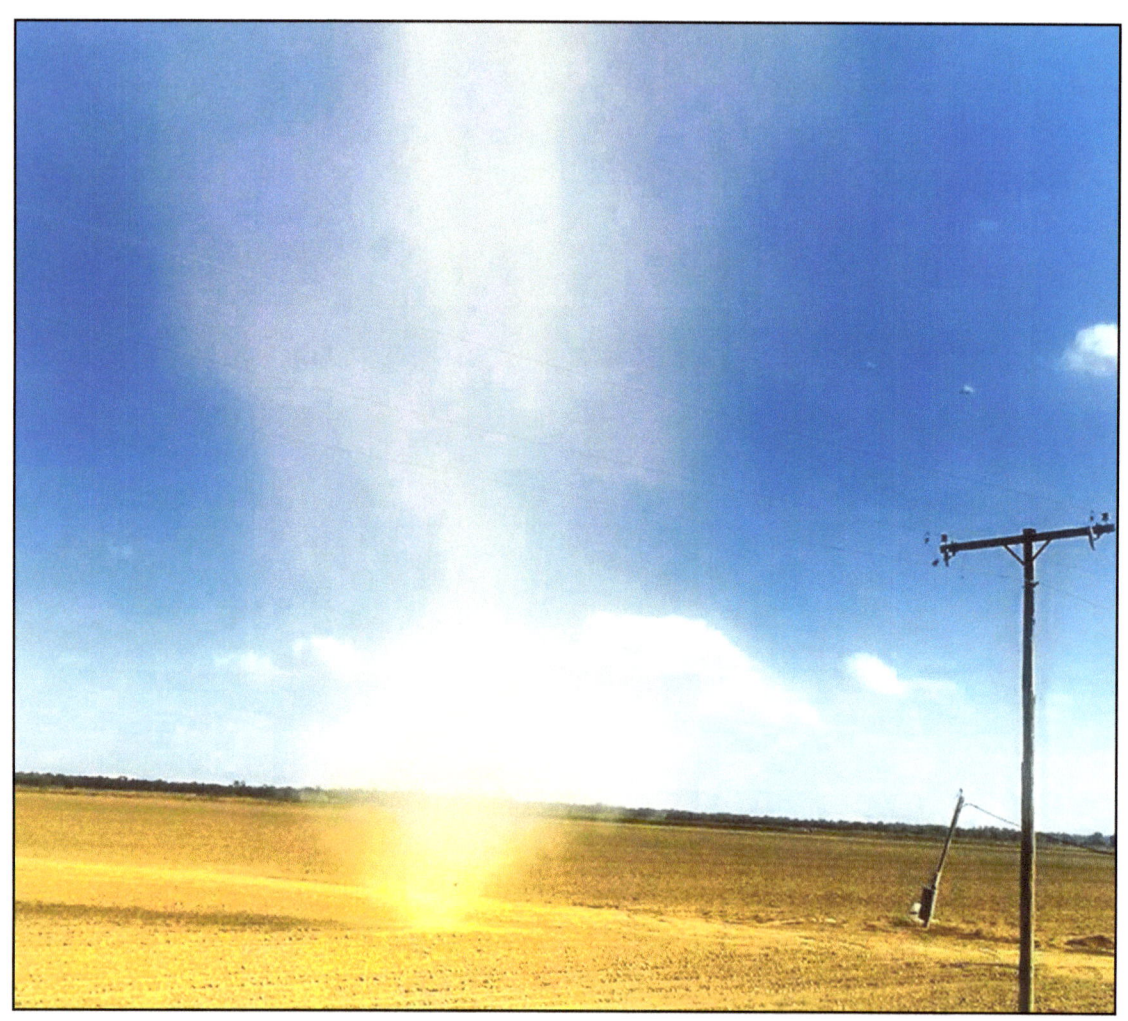

Dust Devil, Lake Providence, Louisiana

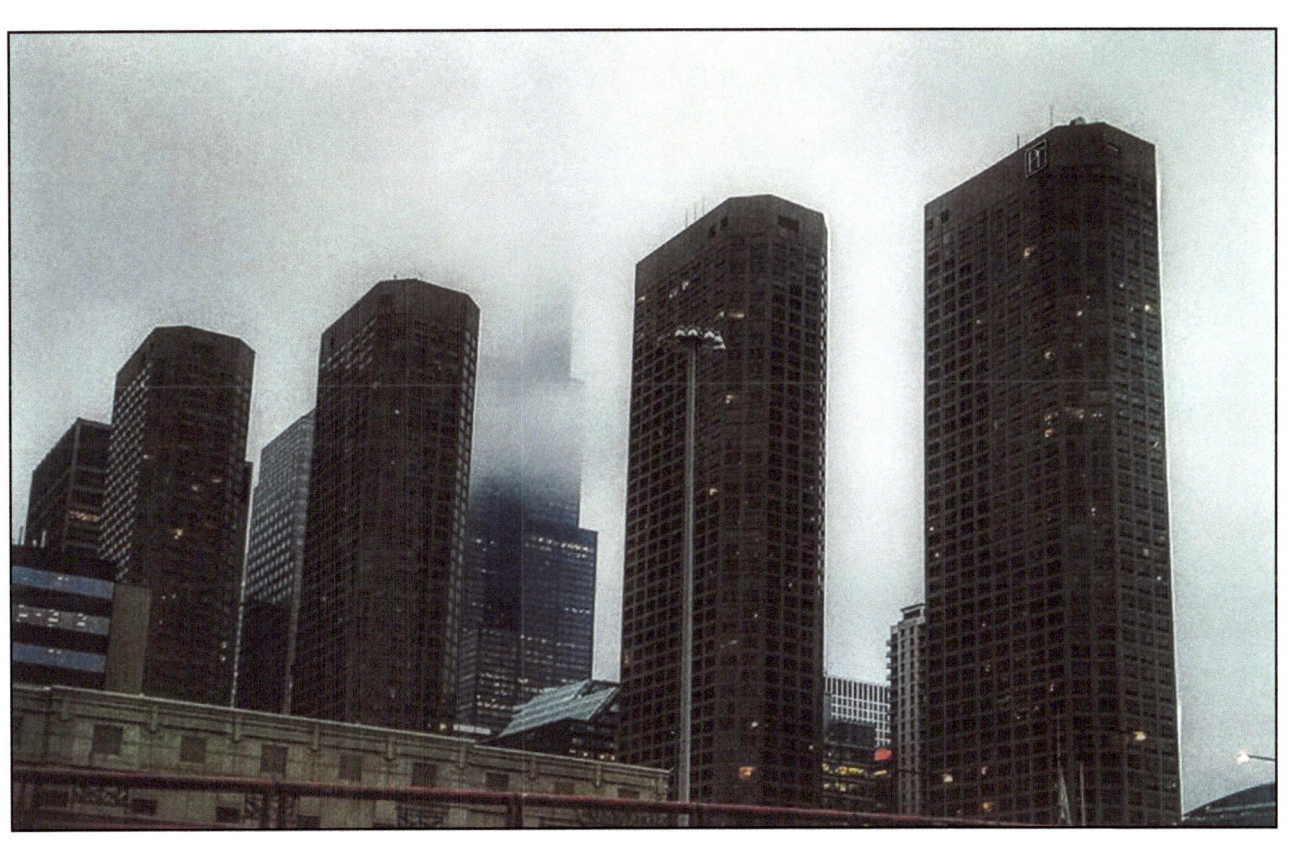

Chicago, Illinois
The Willis Tower is mostly hidden by the low clouds .

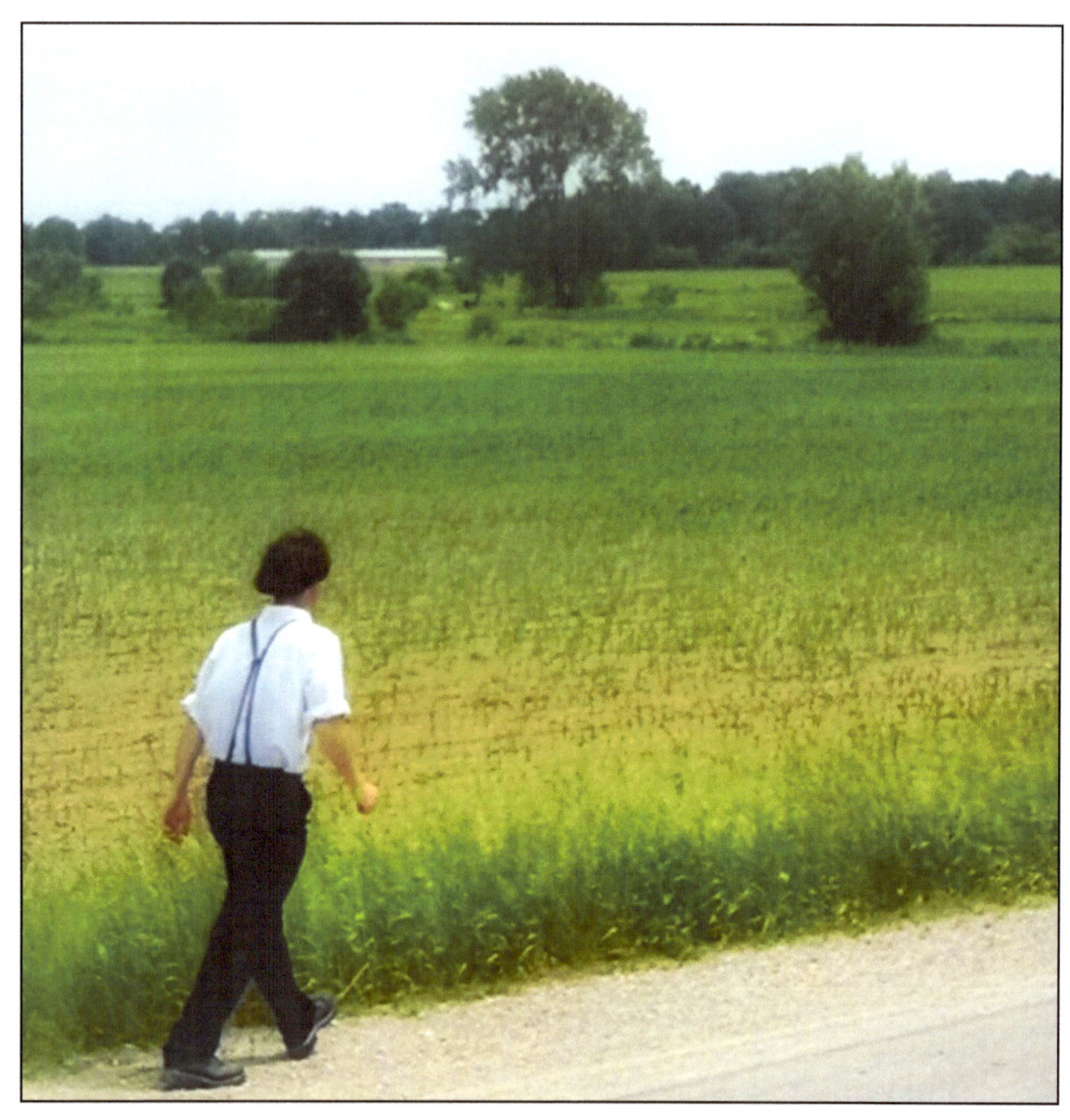

Berne, Indiana

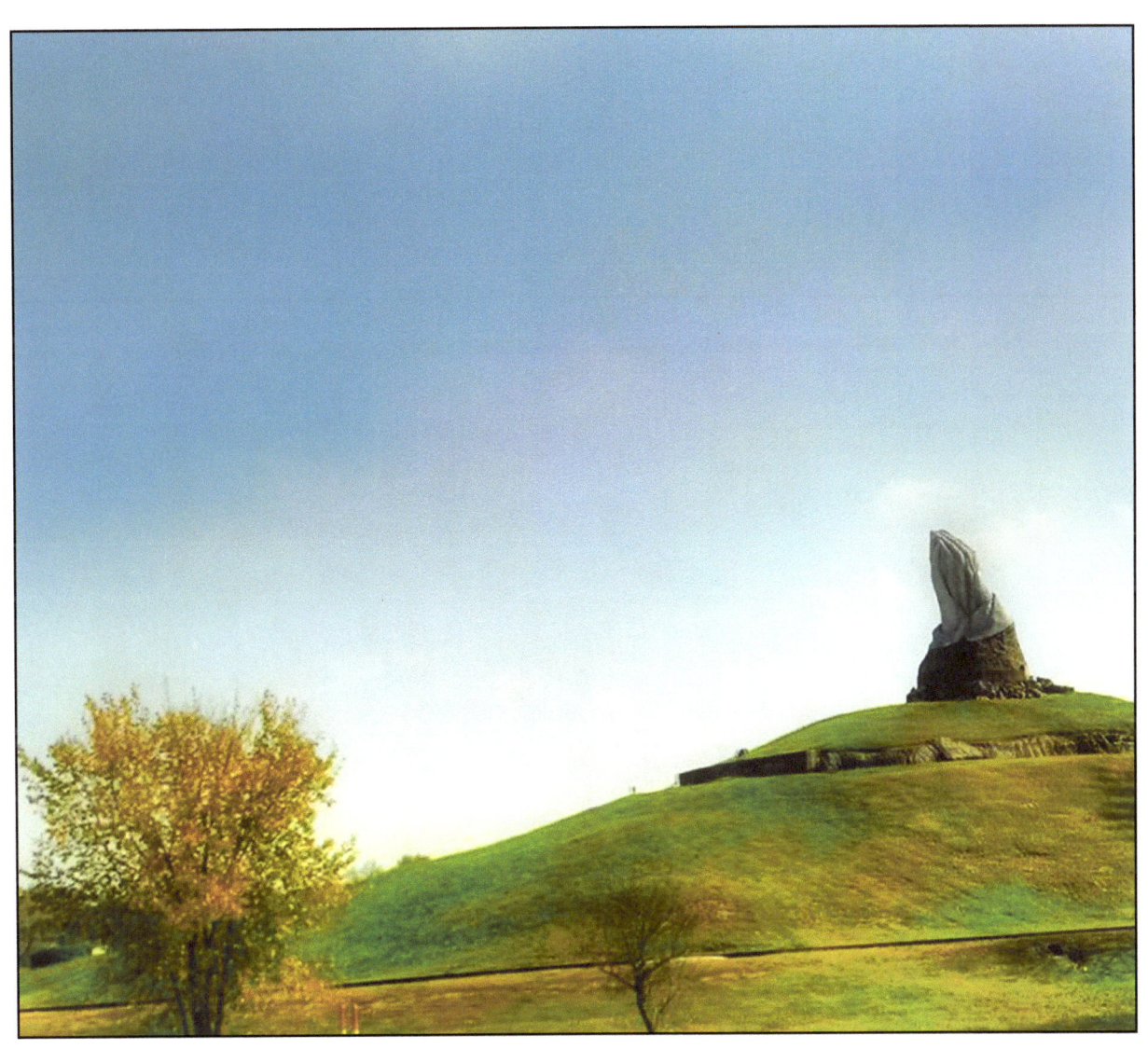

Webb City, Missouri - Praying Hands
They were sculpted by local artist J.E. "Jack" Dawson in 1972

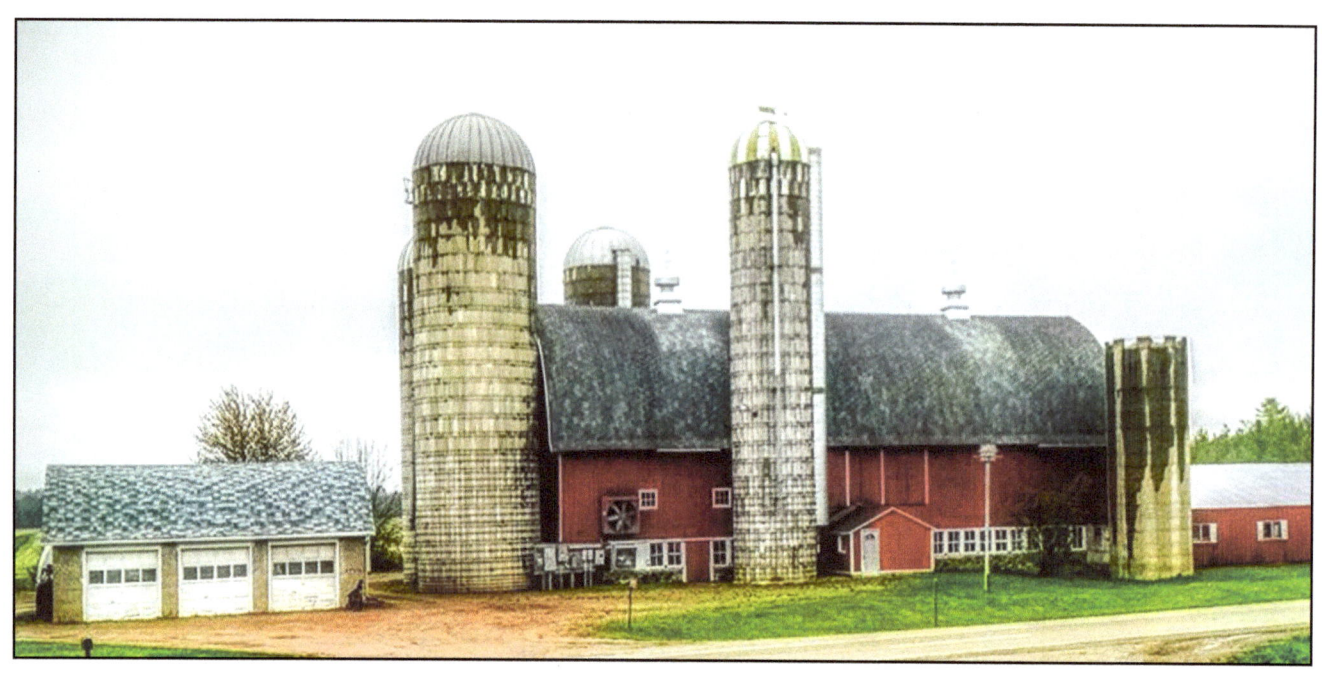

Wisconsin Dairy Farm

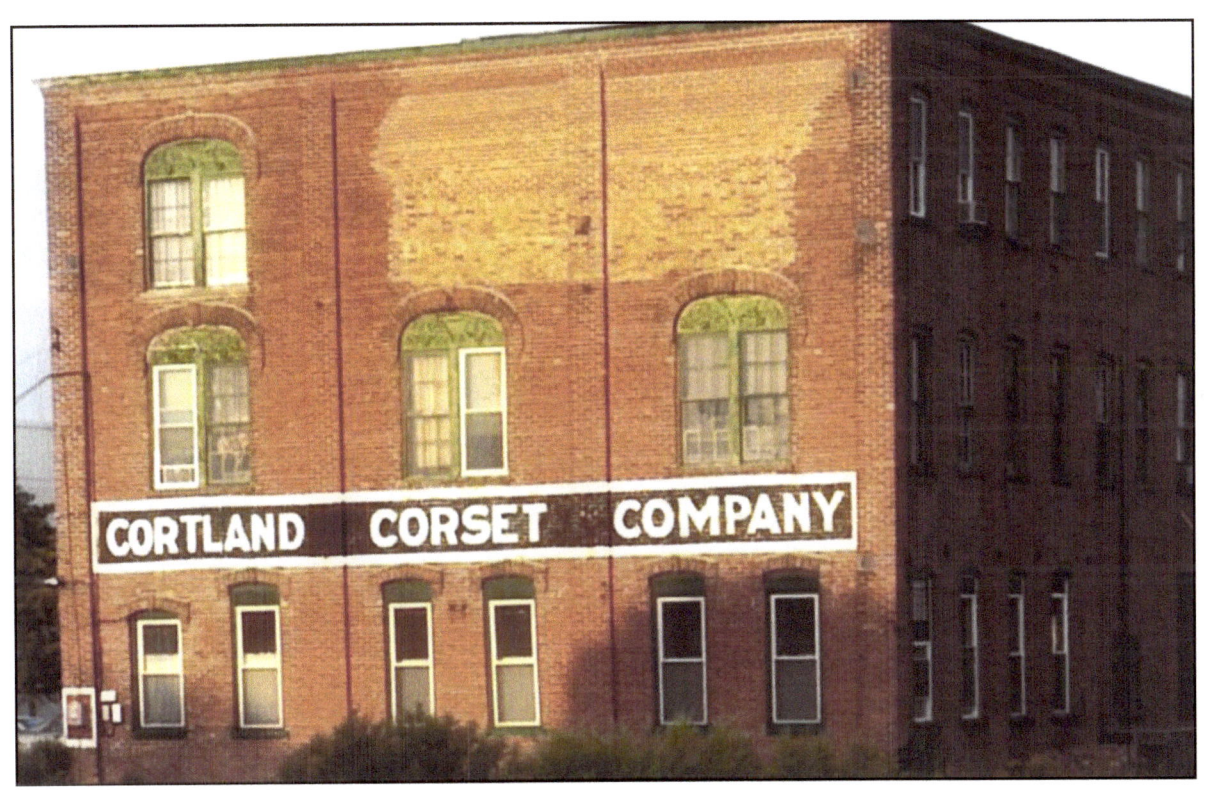

Courtland, New York
Built in 1872 by the Cortland Wagon Company

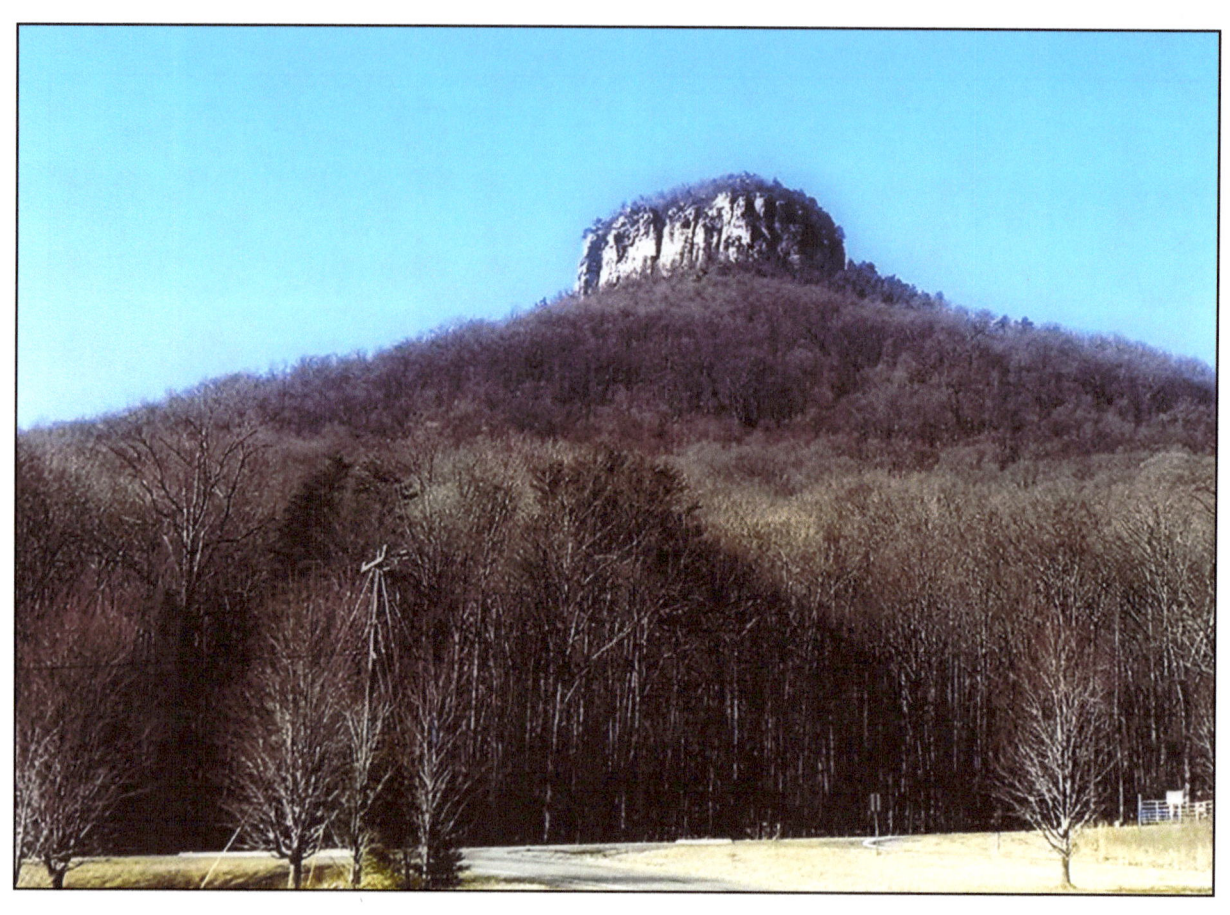

Pilot Mountain, North Carolina
Rising abruptly more than 2,000 feet, Pilot Mountain has been a navigational landmark for centuries.

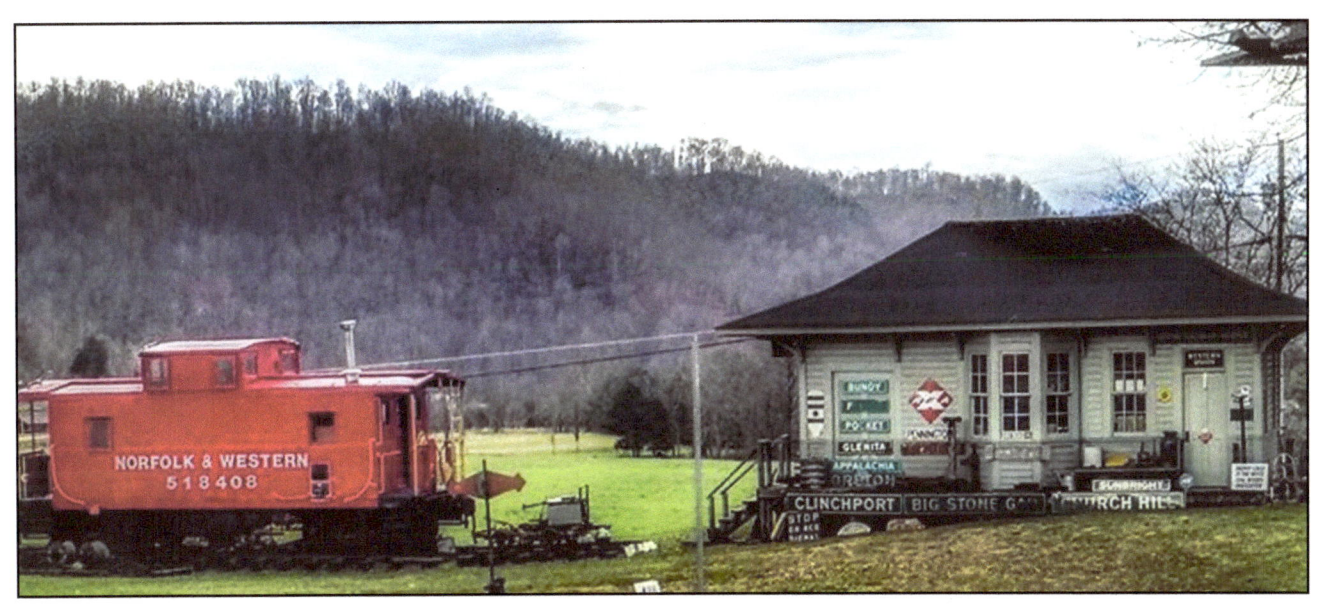

Duffield, Virginia
The depot was used as a prop in the movie, "Coal Miner's Daughter.
Kenny Fannon and his grandson, Ruston Fannon, are preserving the history of the railroad in
Southwest Virginia. They currently have refurbished an authentic N&W Railroad caboose, a diesel engine
from Blue Diamond Coal Company in Scotia, KY, and a tender car from ETW & NC called the Tweetsie Line.

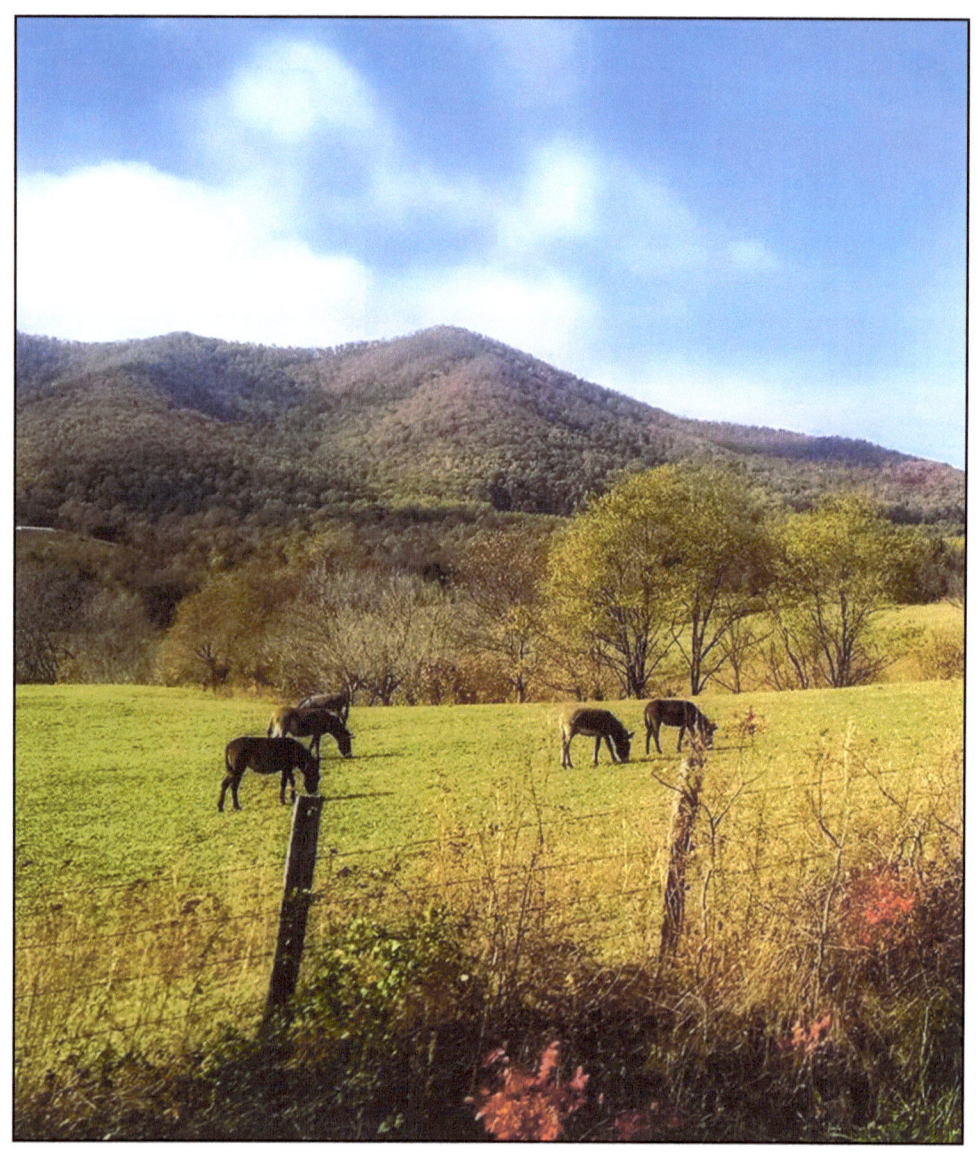

Big Island, Virginia

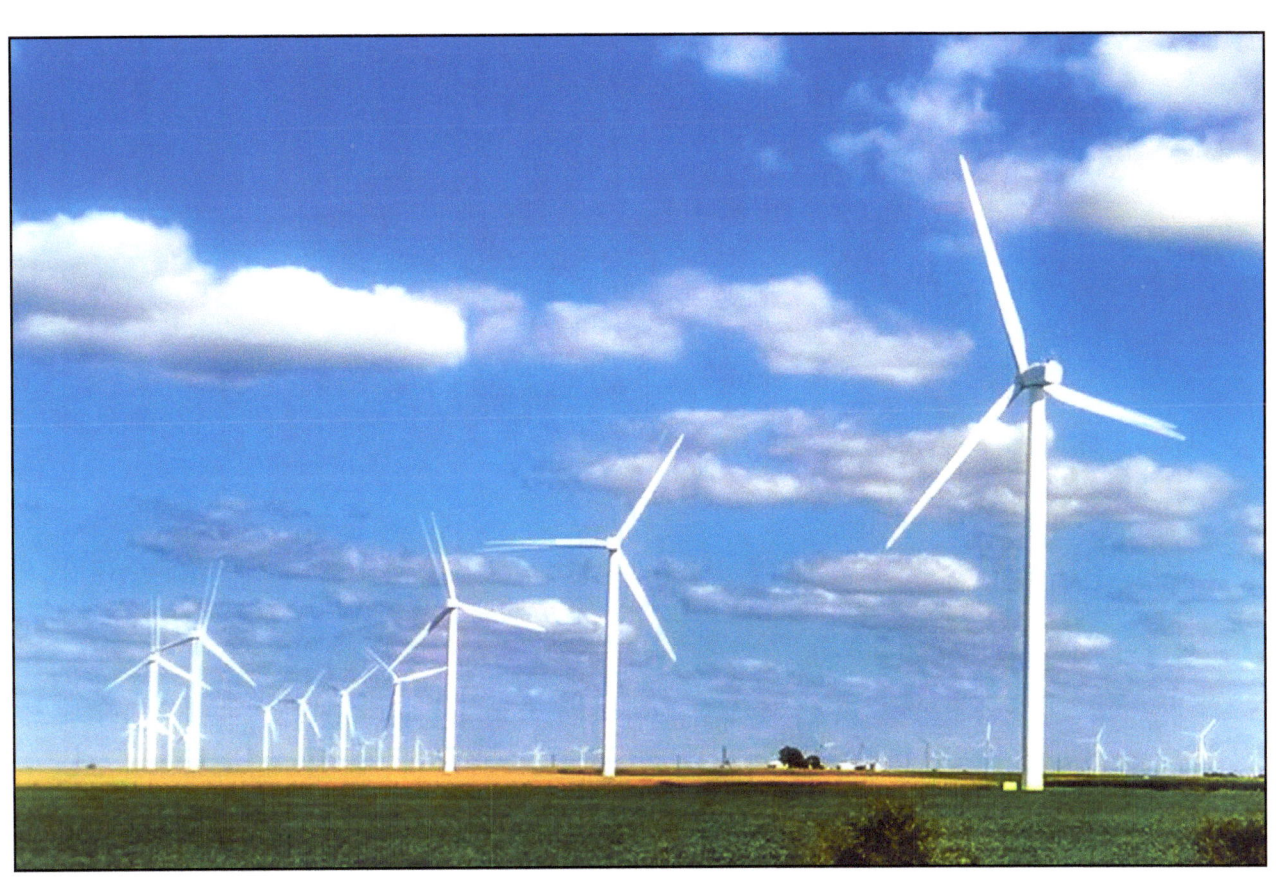

Northern Illinois Wind Farm
Typical of the many wind farm across the midwestern plains.

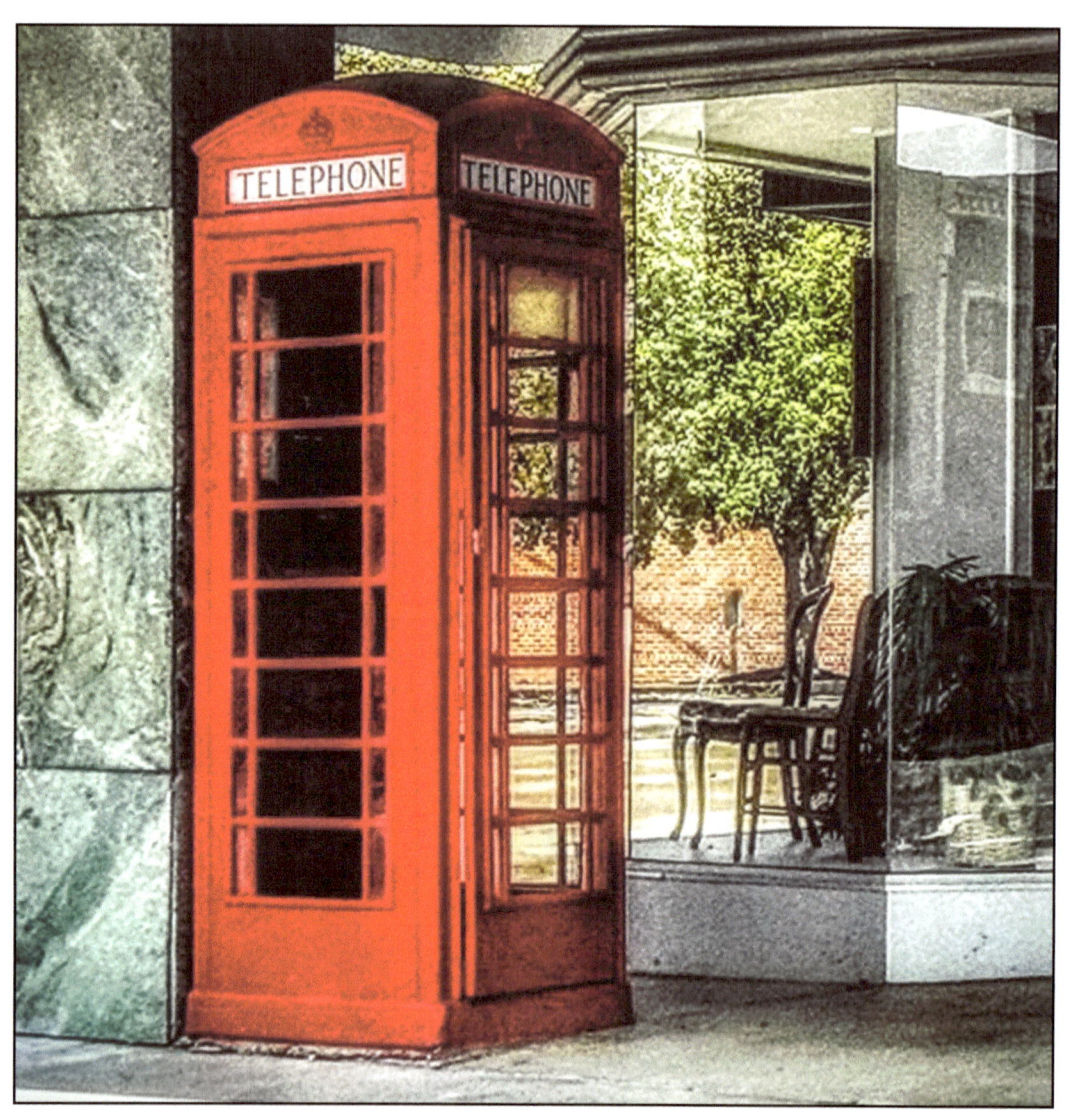

Kingsport, Tennessee
Local business man Norman Sobel had the British telephone booth installed in front of his store in the downtown area. When he retired and the business closed, the booth remained.

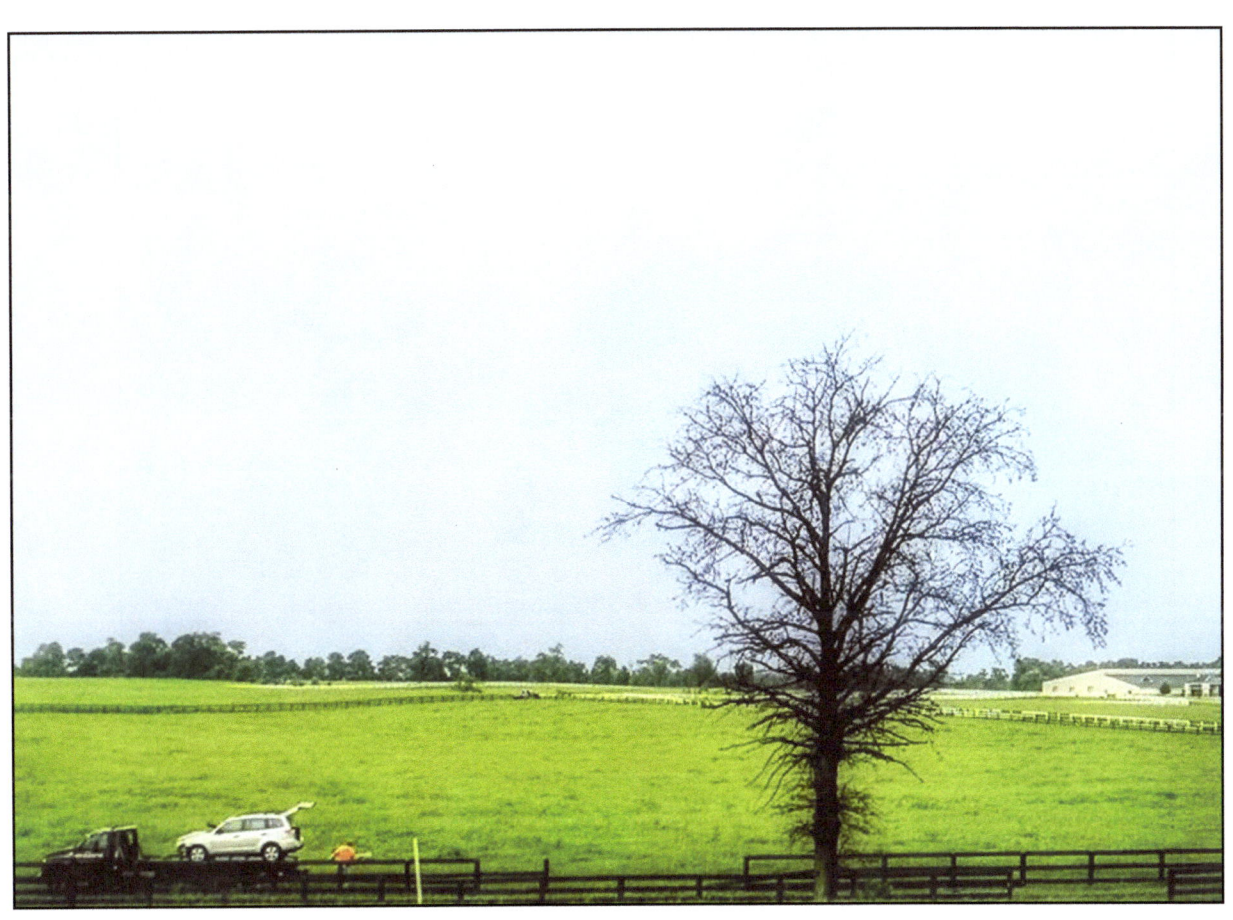

Lexington, Kentucky

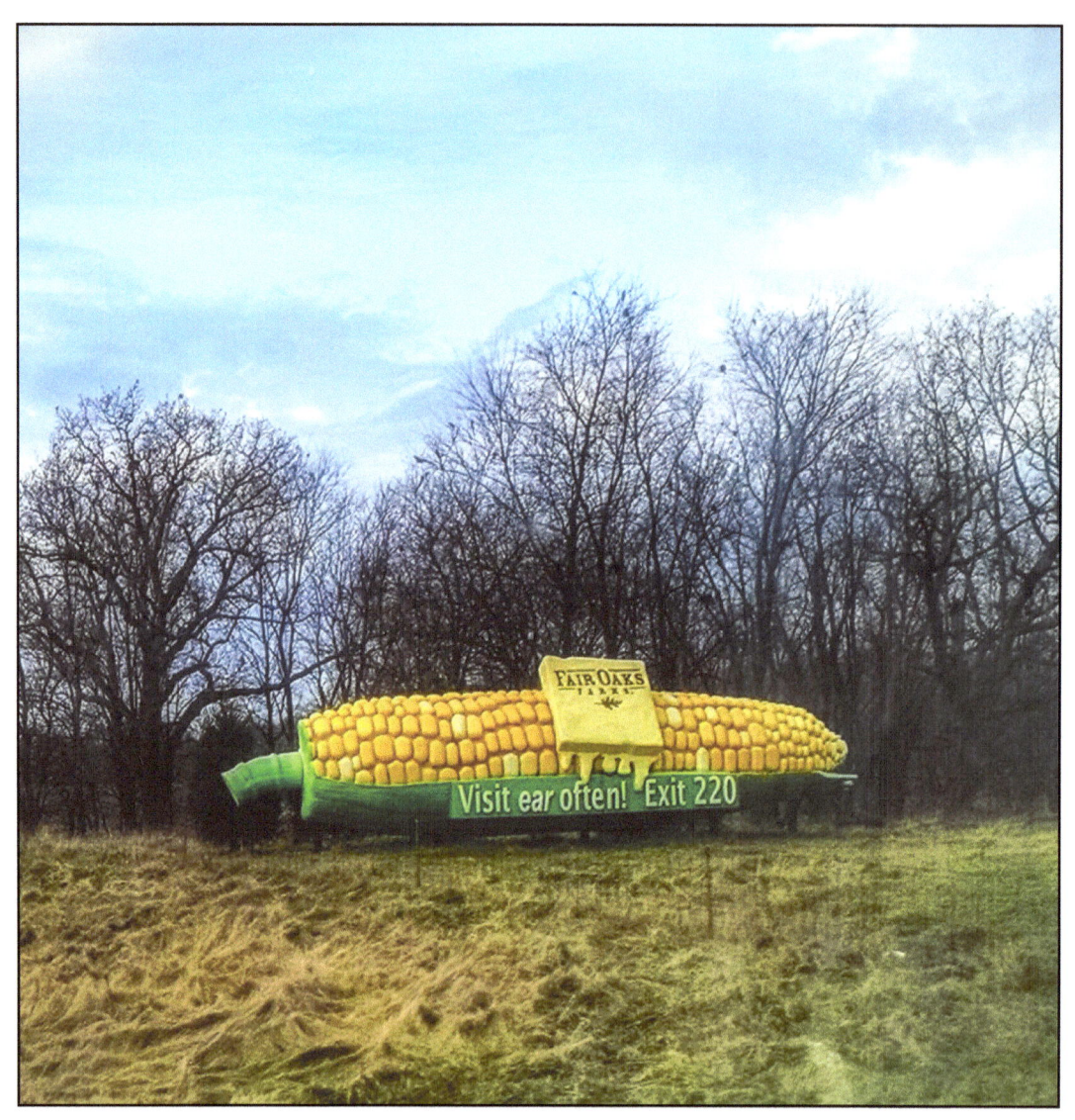

Fair Oaks, Indiana
The giant ear of corn and large fork are advertising promotions for Fair Oaks Farms.

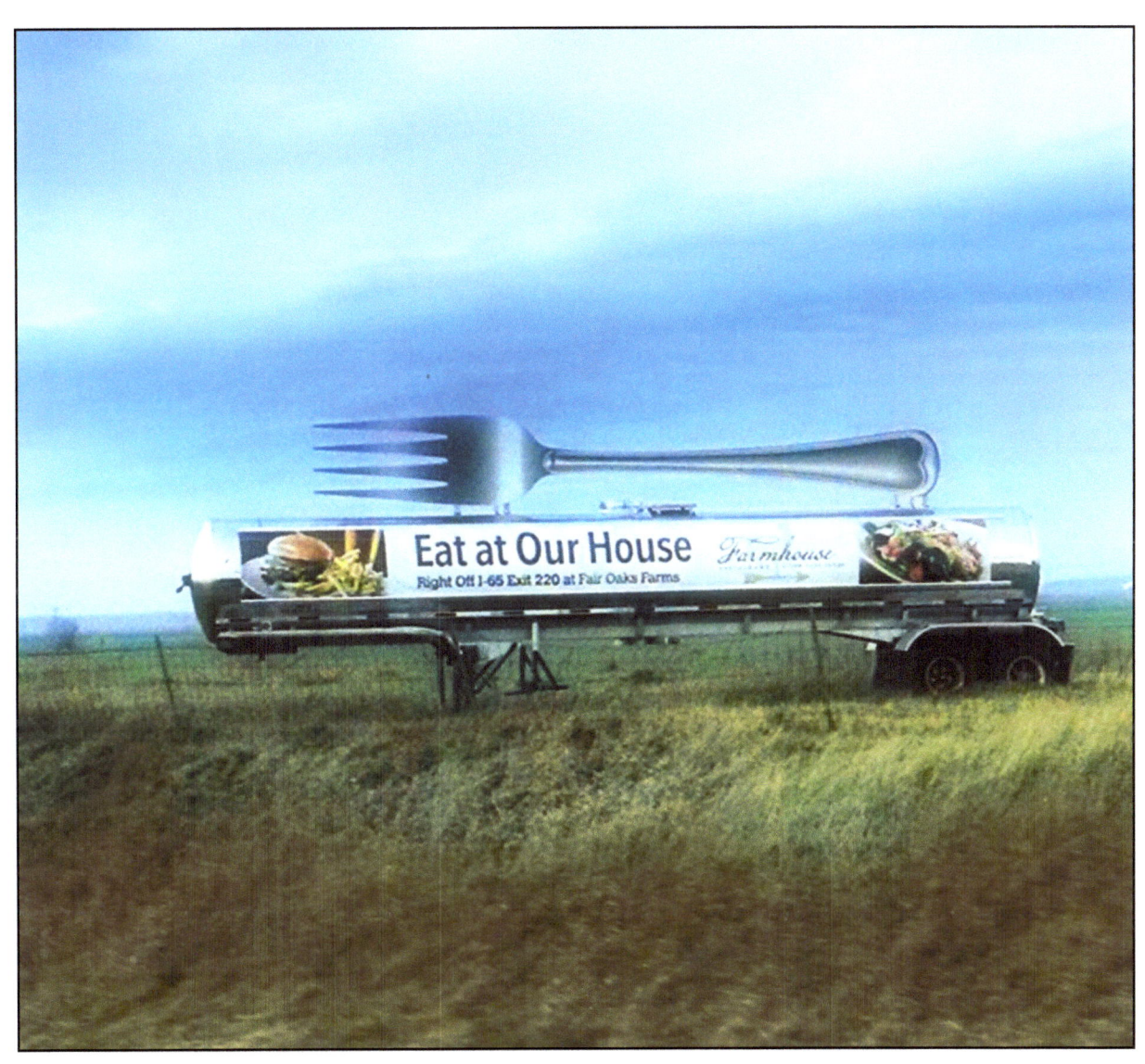

Fair Oaks, Indiana
Fair Oaks Farms Restaurant off Interstate 65 serves 800-1200 customers a day

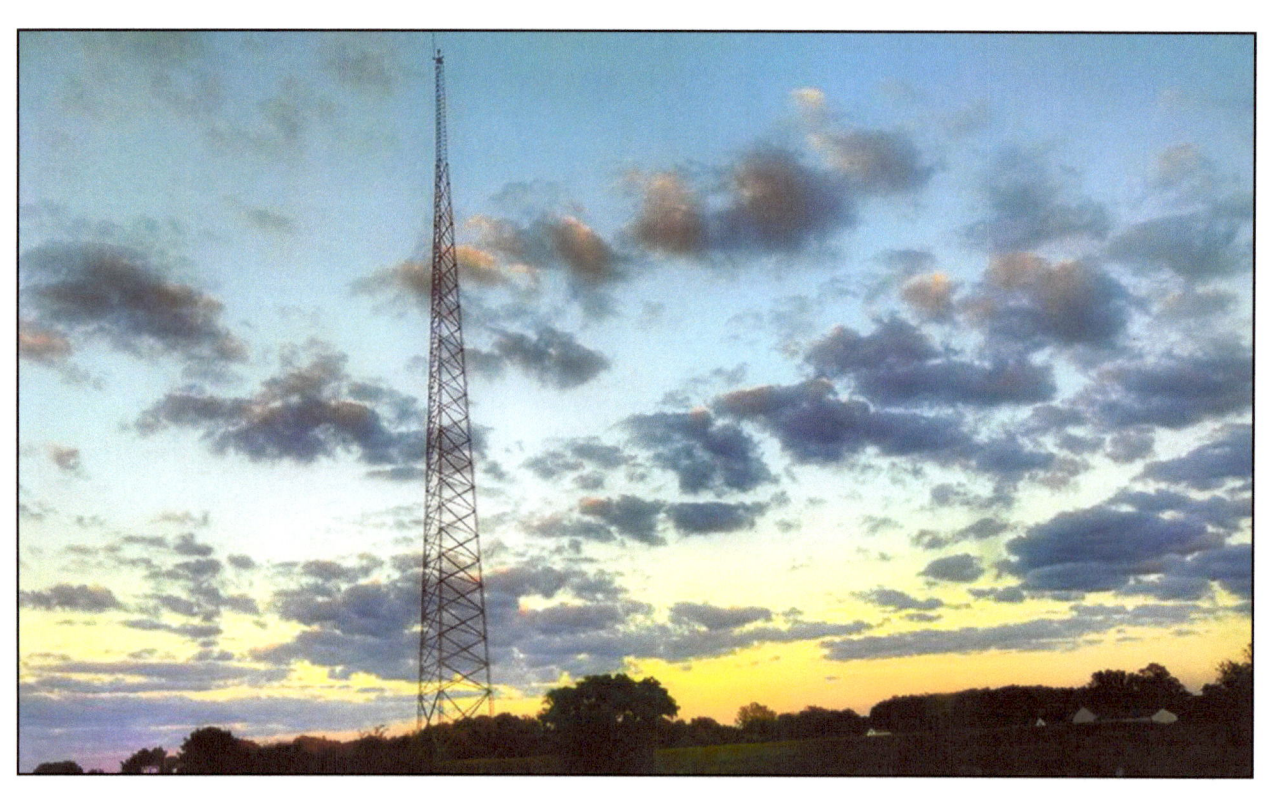

Saint Leon, Indiana

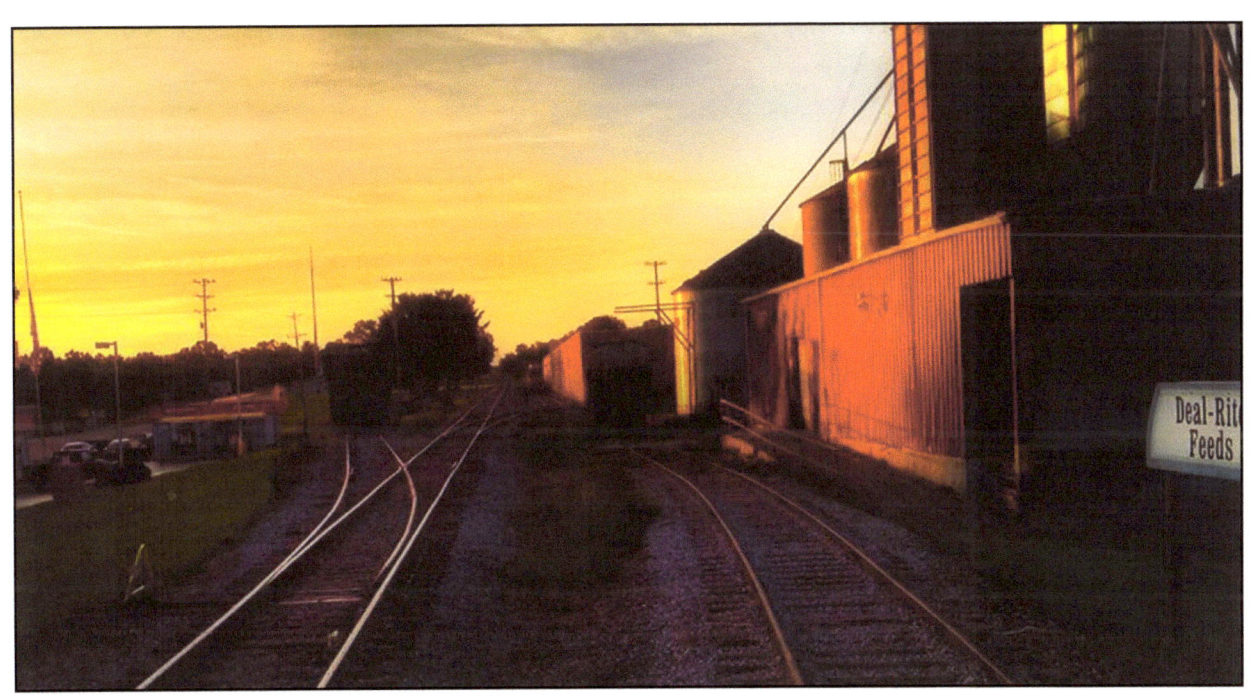

Statesville, North Carolina

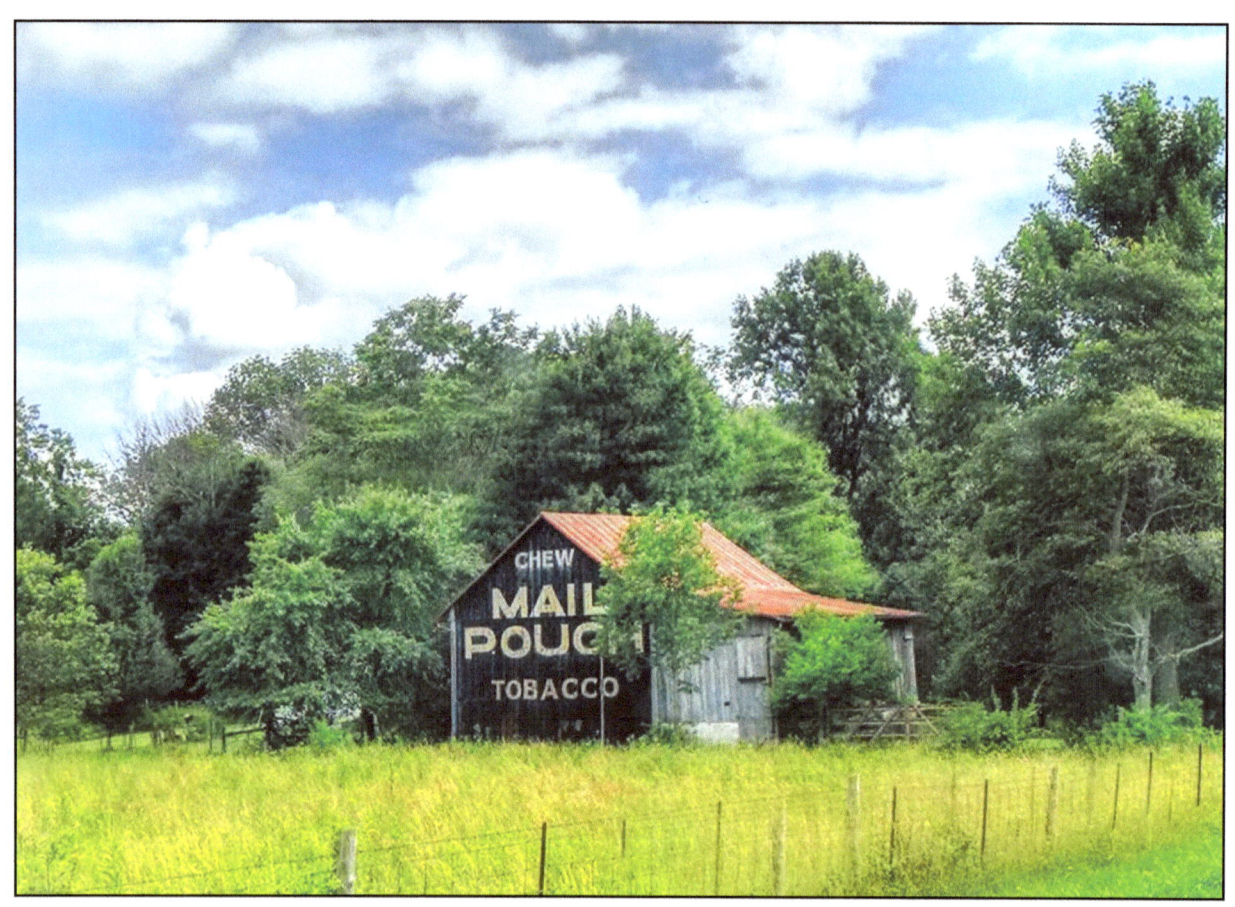

Southern Ohio

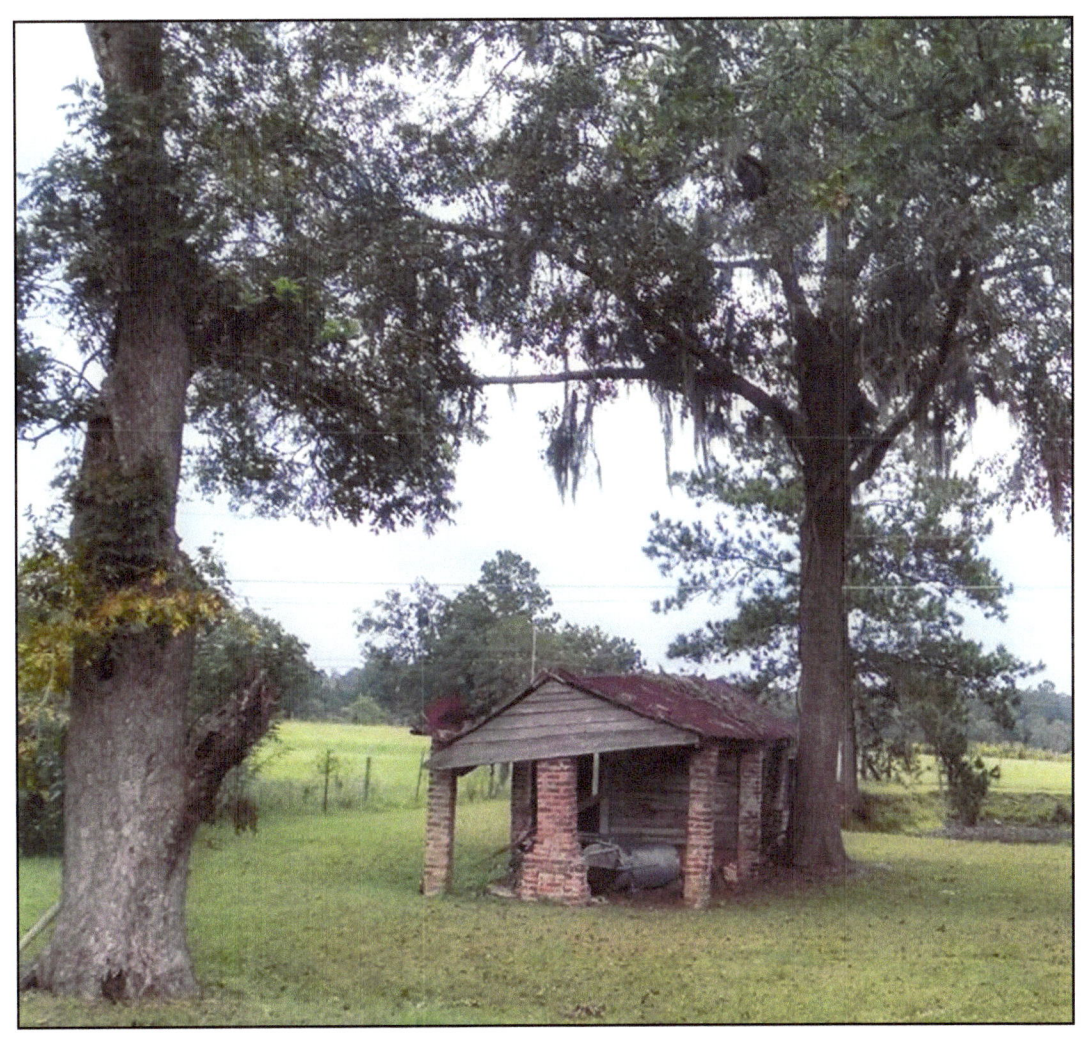

Dasher, Georgia

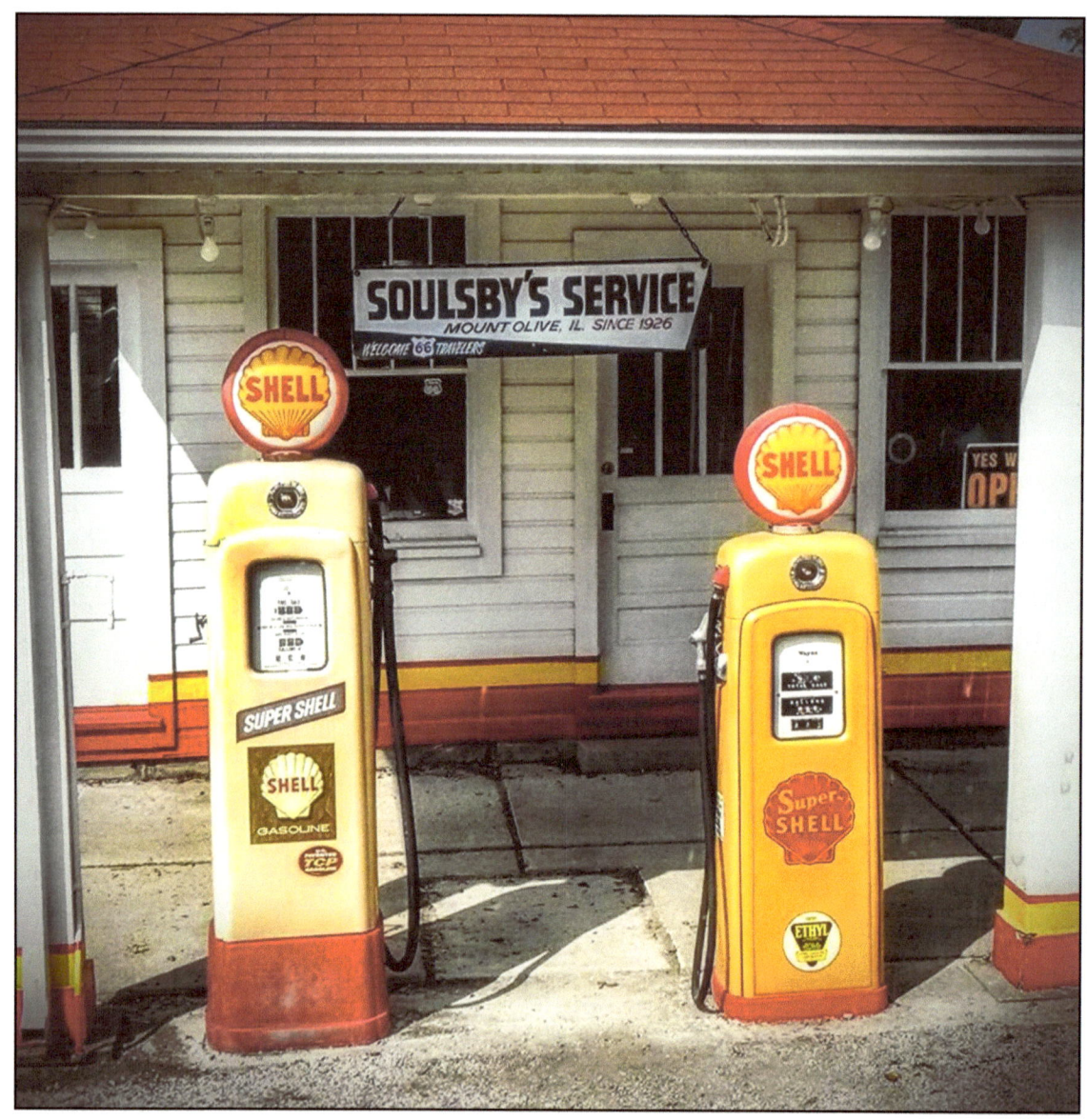

Mount Olive, Illinois

The station is located along historic U.S. Route 66 and is the oldest usable service station on the highway in Illinois. It serves as an example of the house and canopy gas station design. Henry Soulsby built the station in 1926.

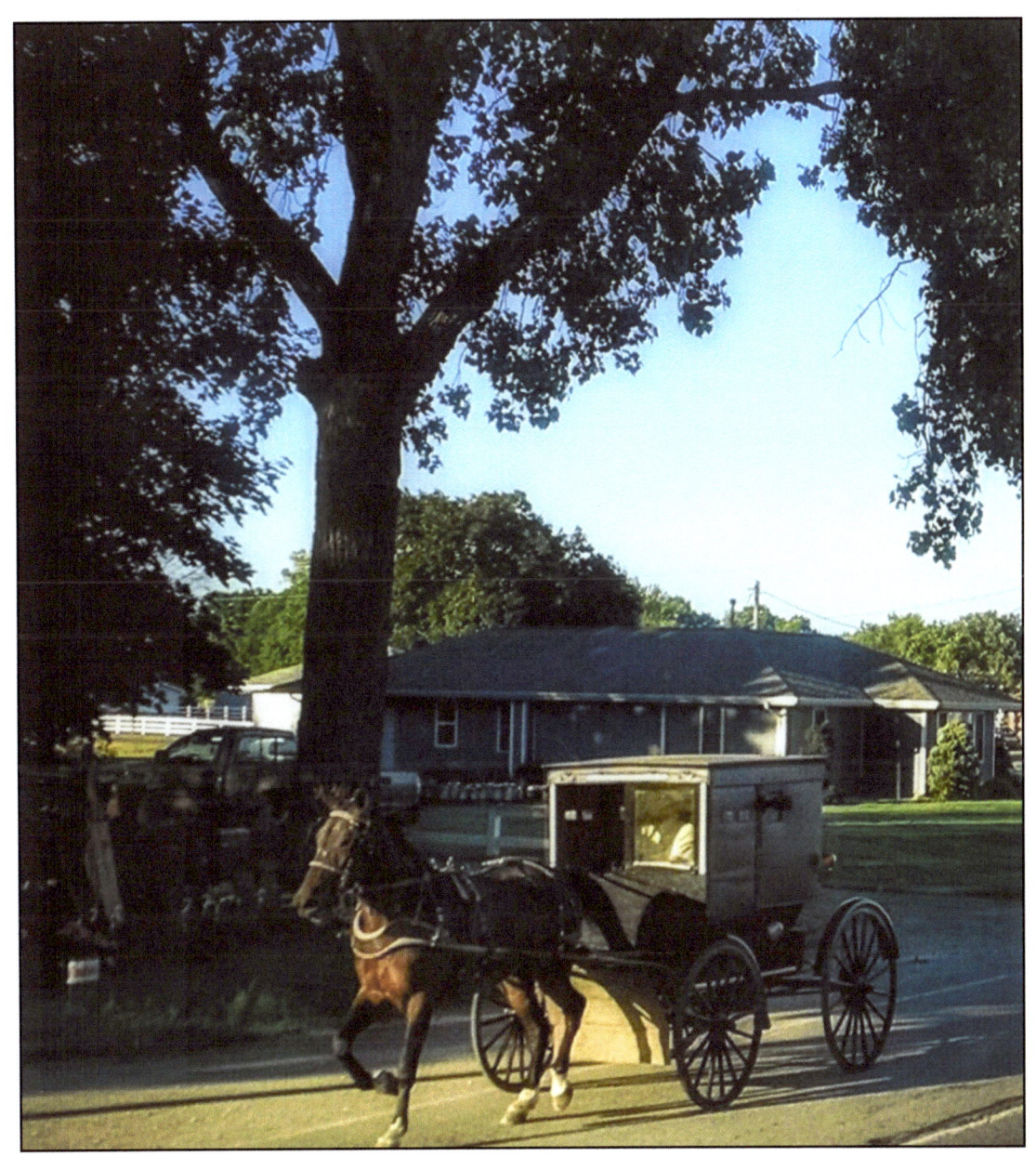

Indiana, Pennsylvania

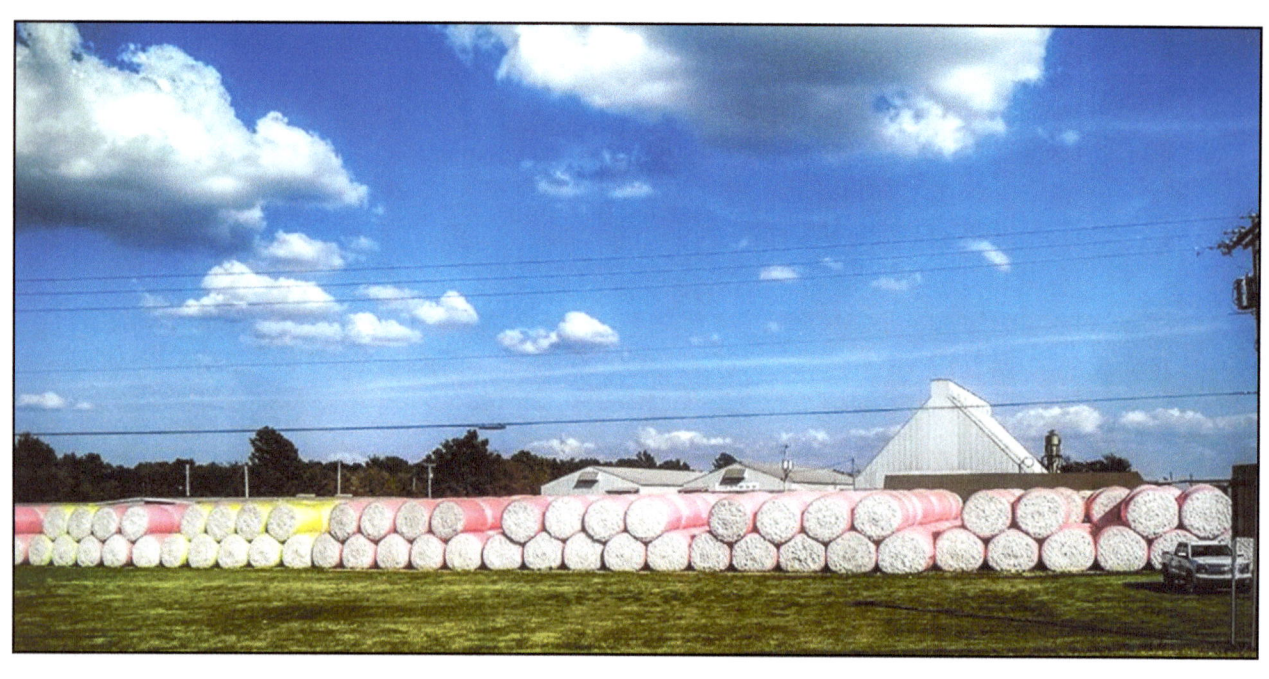

Cotton Bales, Arkansas
See how large the cotton bales are by comparing them to the truck on the right.

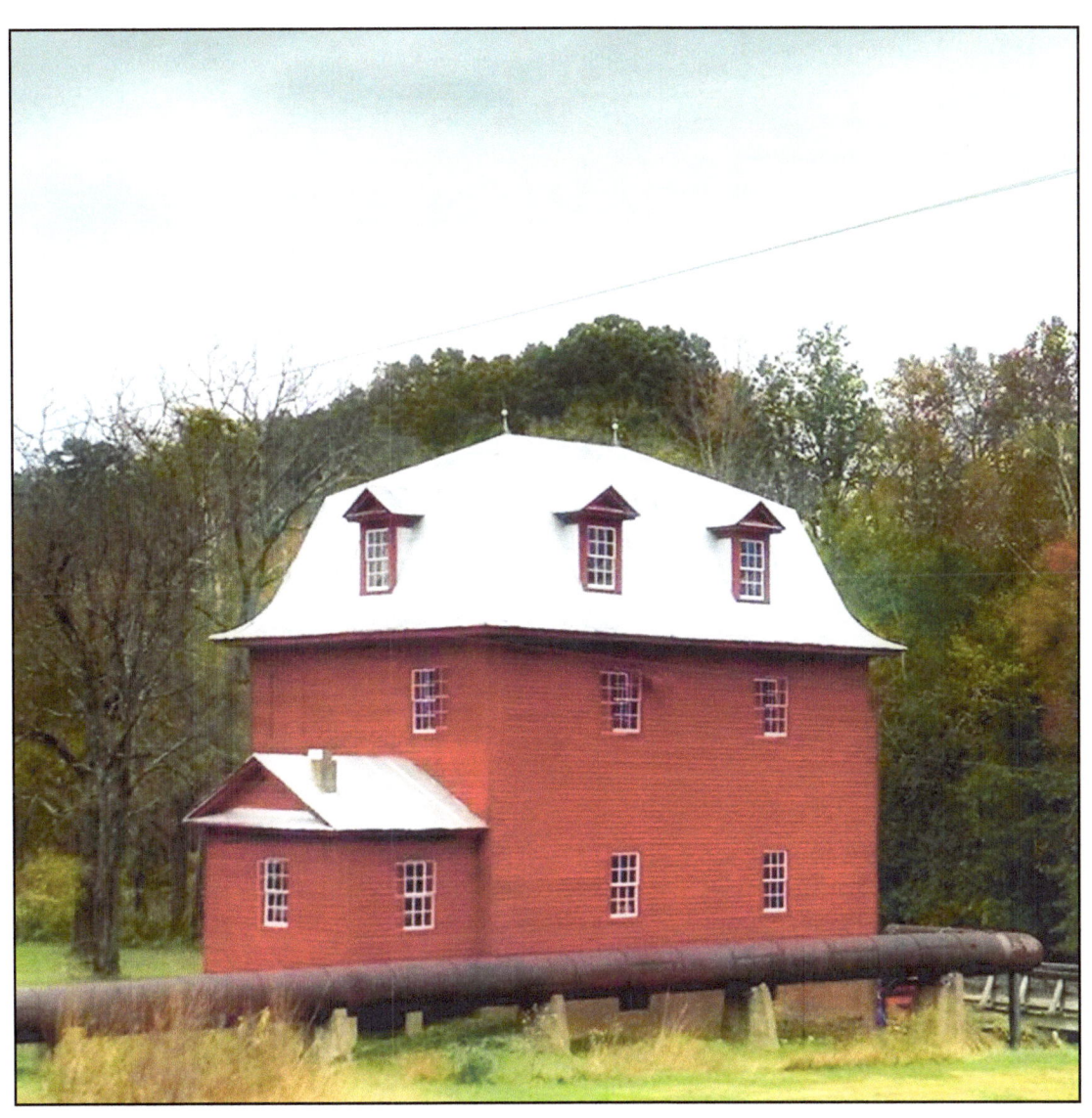

Big Otter River Grist Mill, Bedford County, Virginia
Also known as Forbes Mill, the historic grist mill was built about 1920.

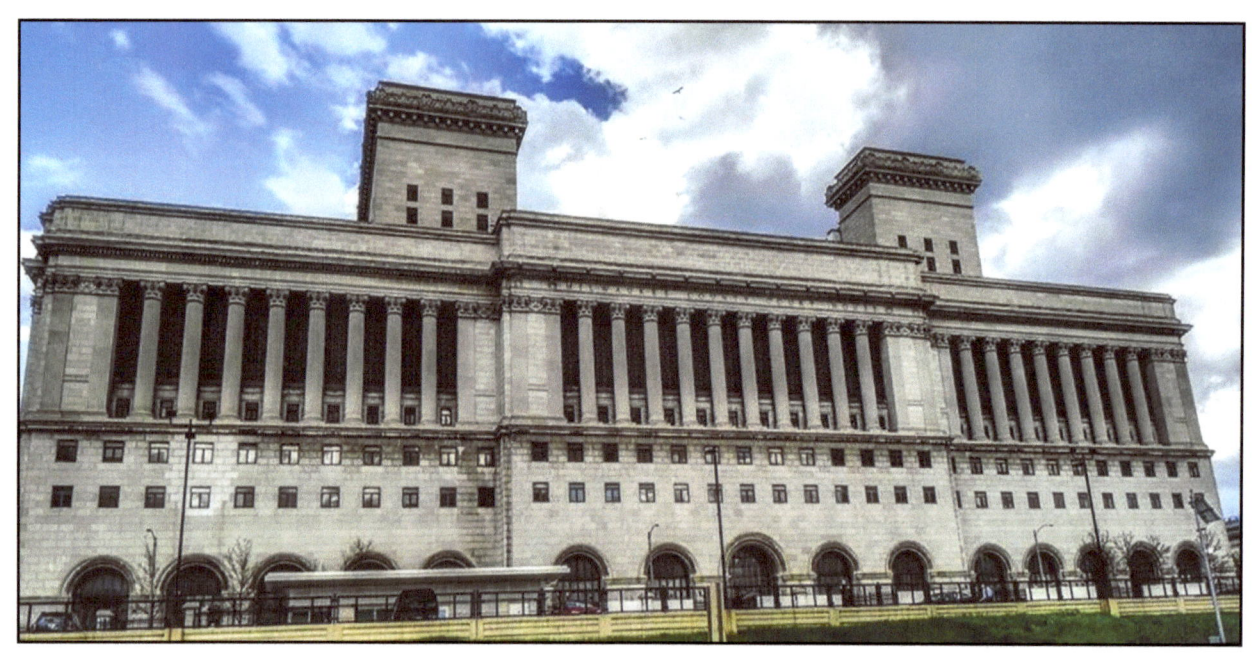

Milwaukee County Courthouse, Wisconsin

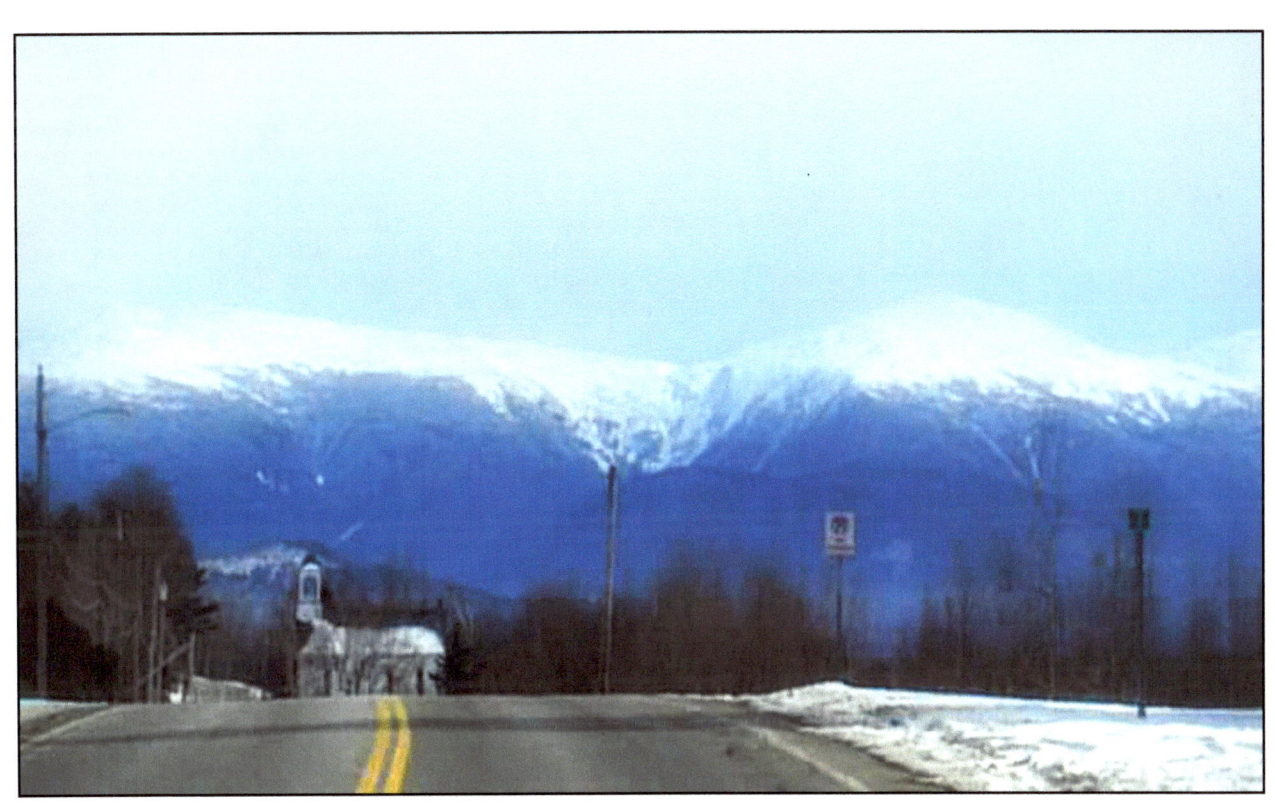

White Mountains, Vermont

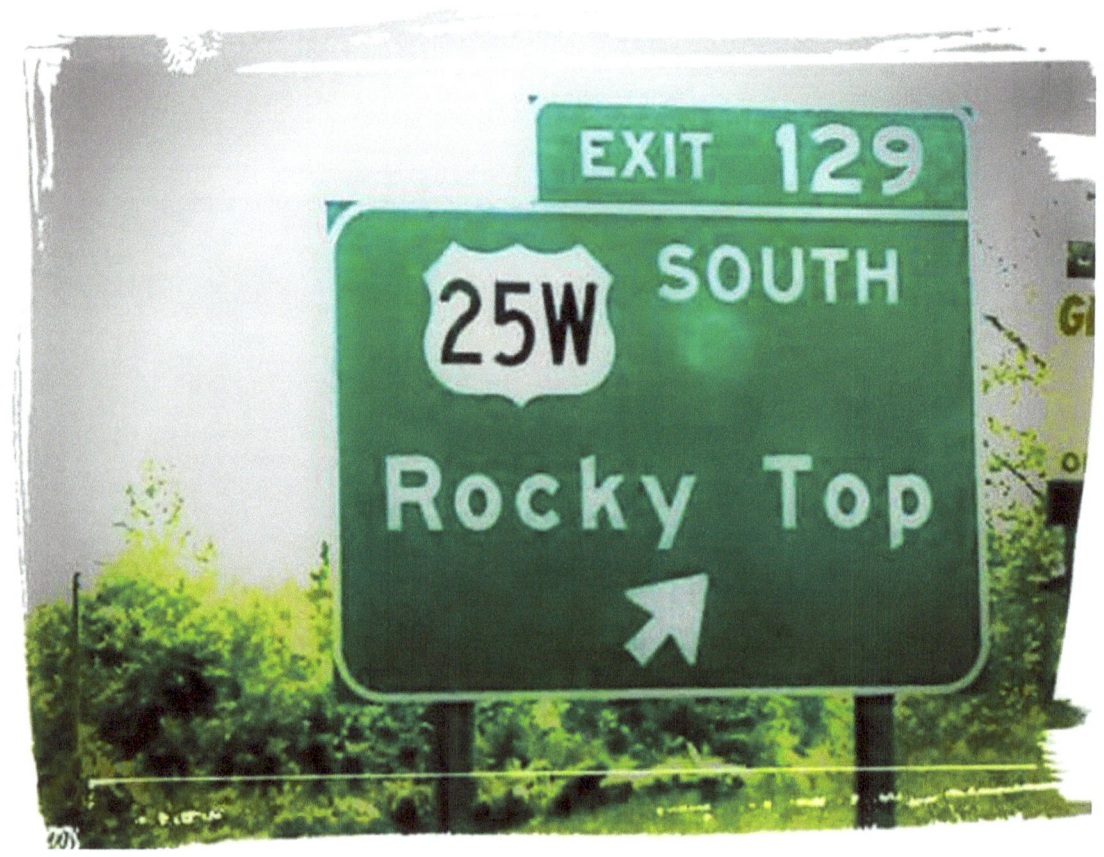

Tennessee....of course!
Rocky Top (formerly Coal Creek and Lake City) is a city in Anderson and Campbell counties northwest of Knoxville. On June 26, 2014, the city officially changed its name from Lake City to Rocky Top.

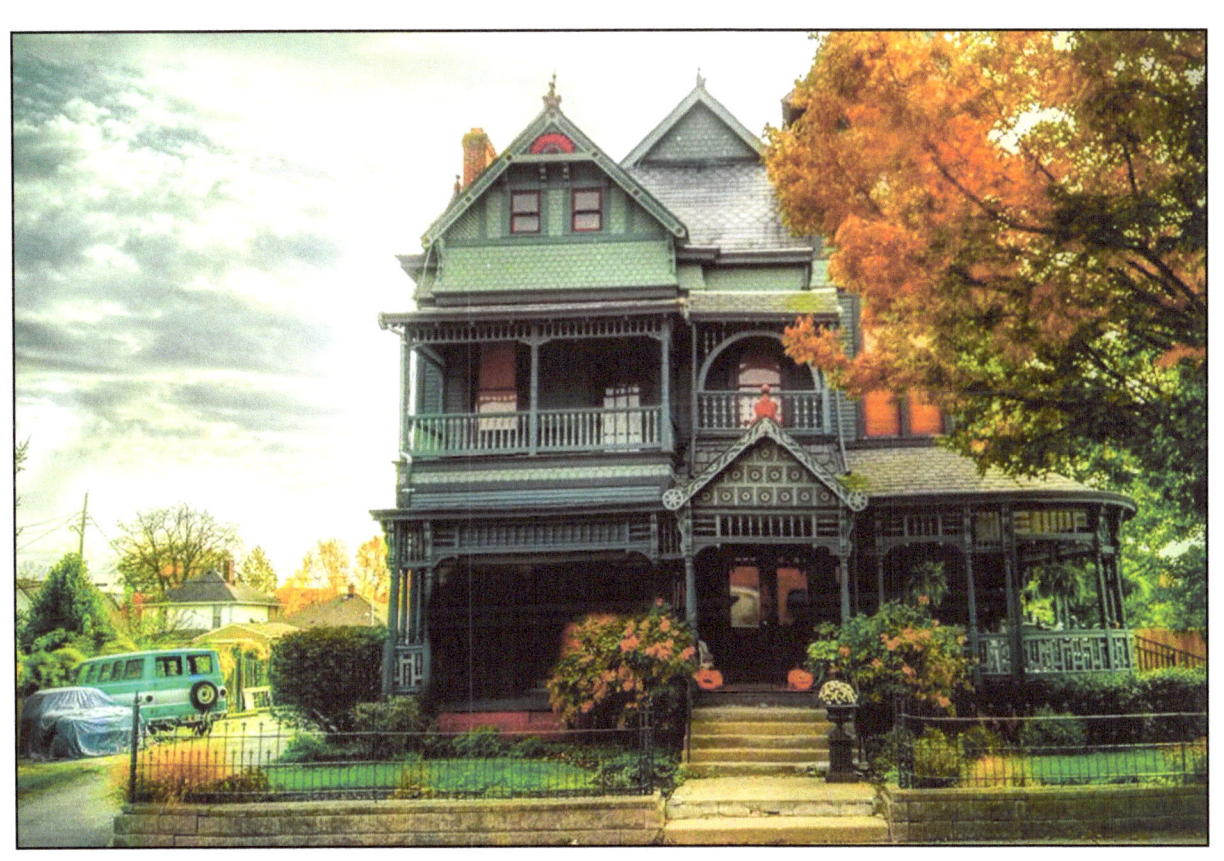

Noblesville, Indiana
A restored Victorian style house.

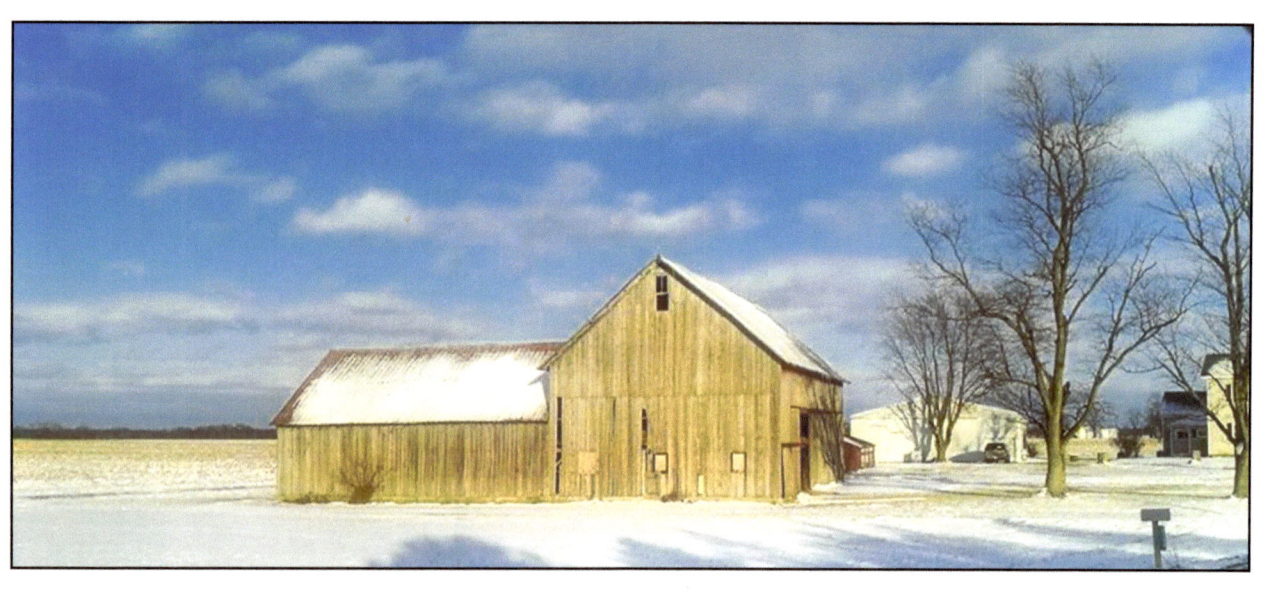

Wilshire, Ohio

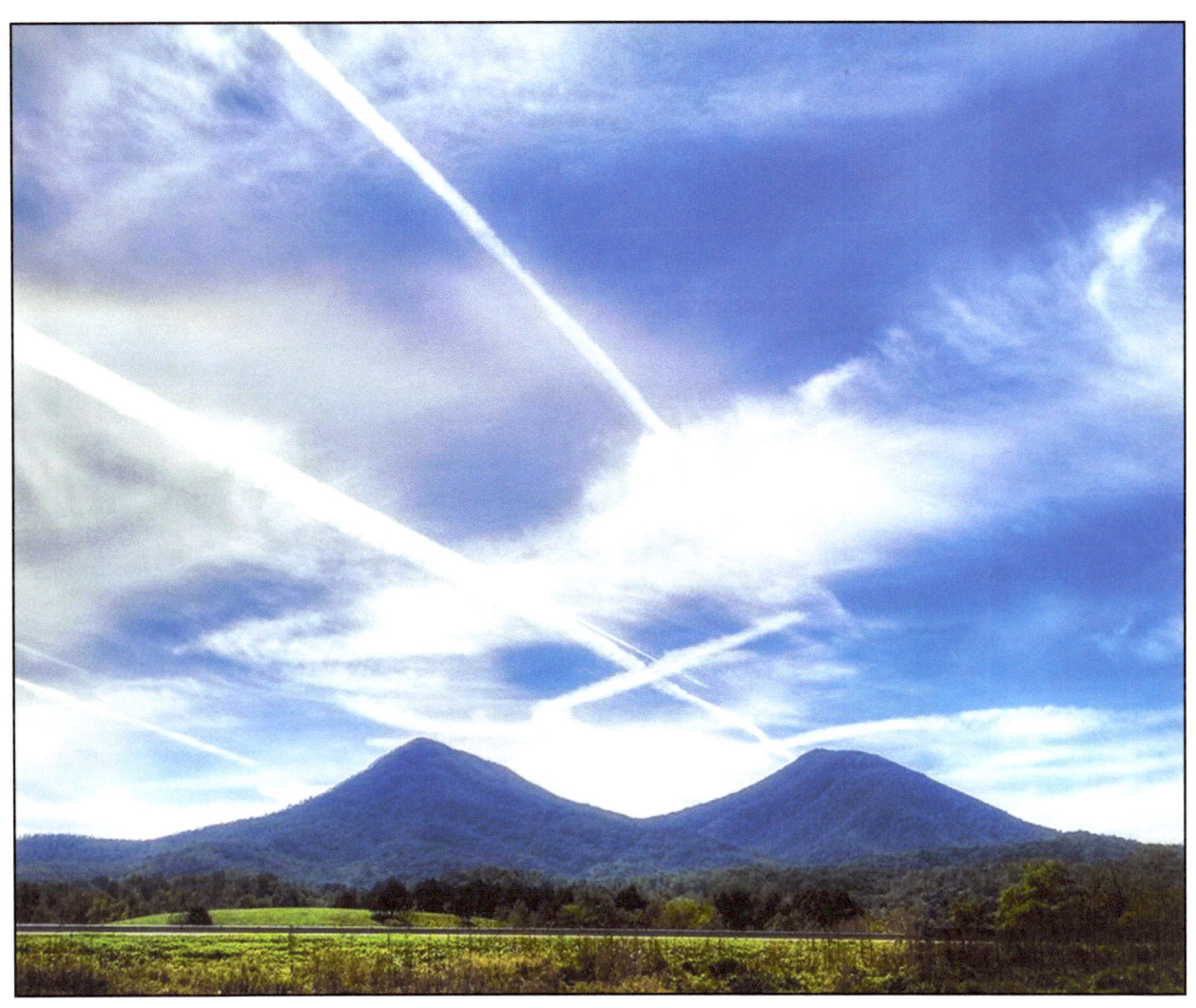

Blue Ridge Mountains, Virginia

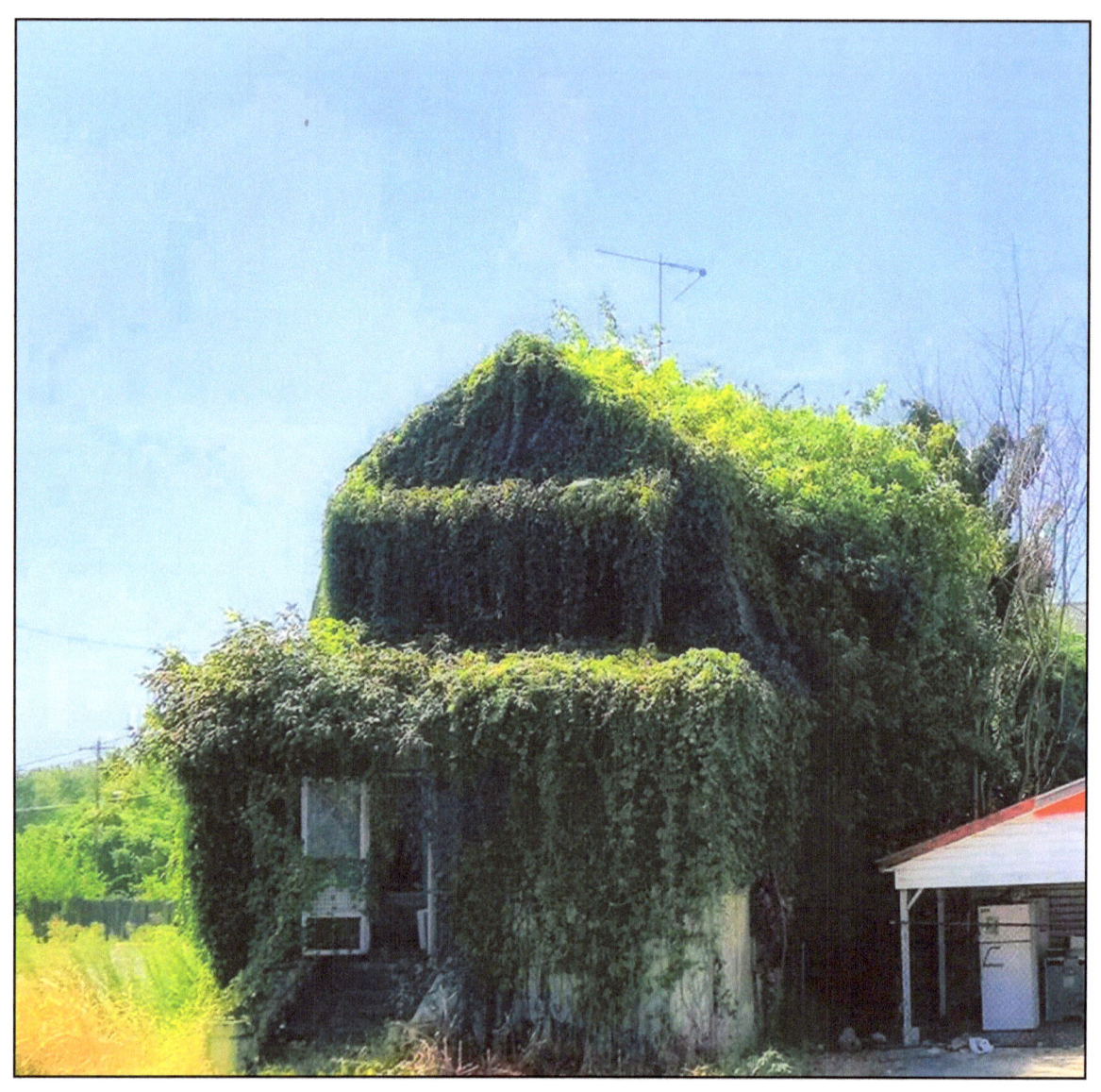

Southern Illinois

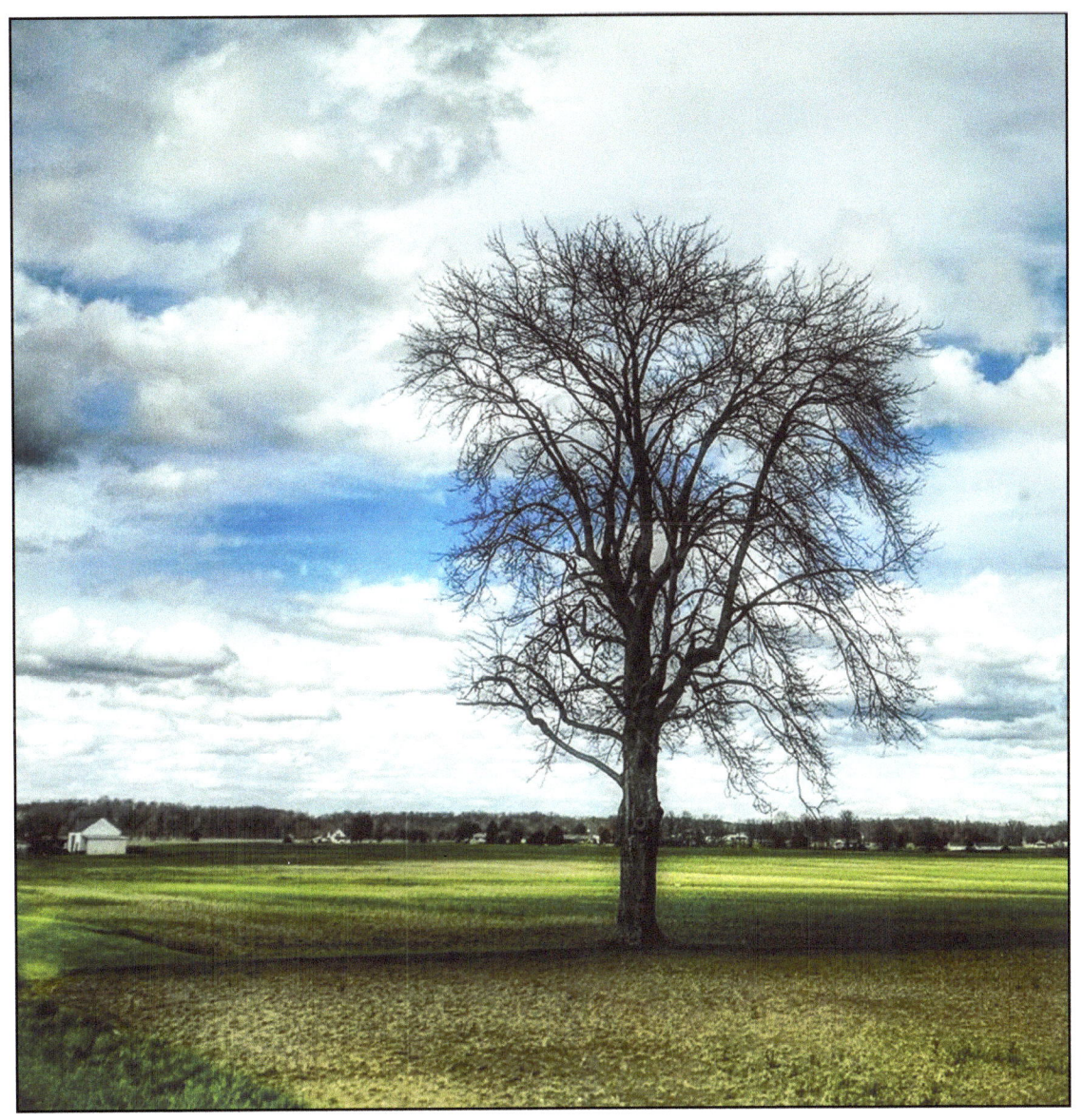

Sunman, Indiana

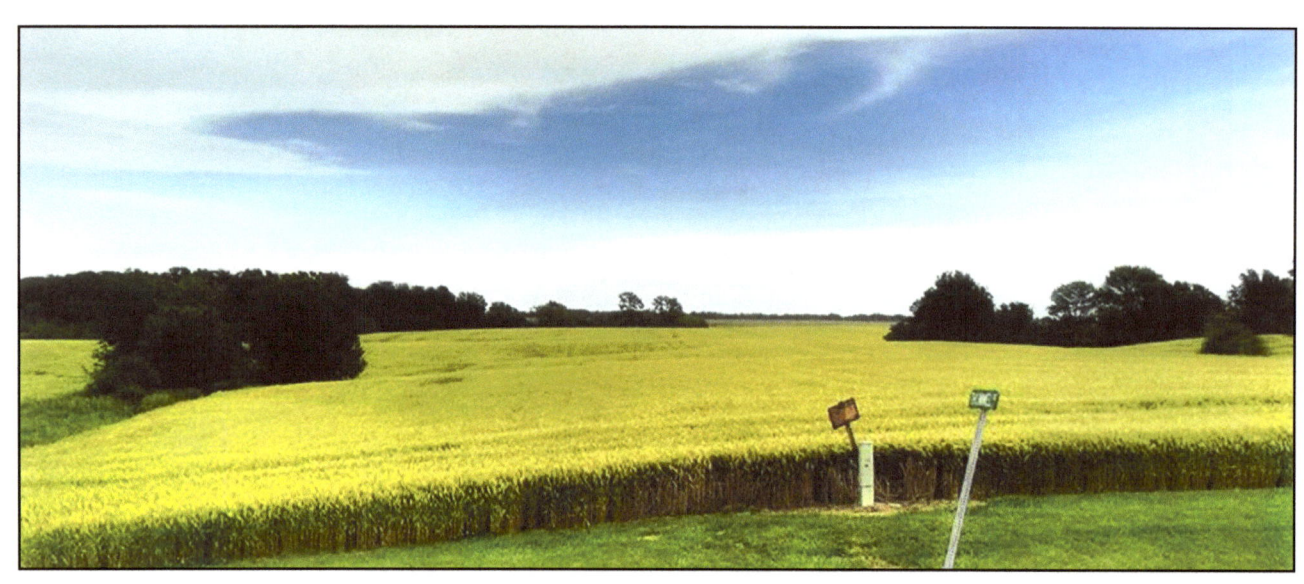

Red Bud, Illinois
A test field of hybrid corn.

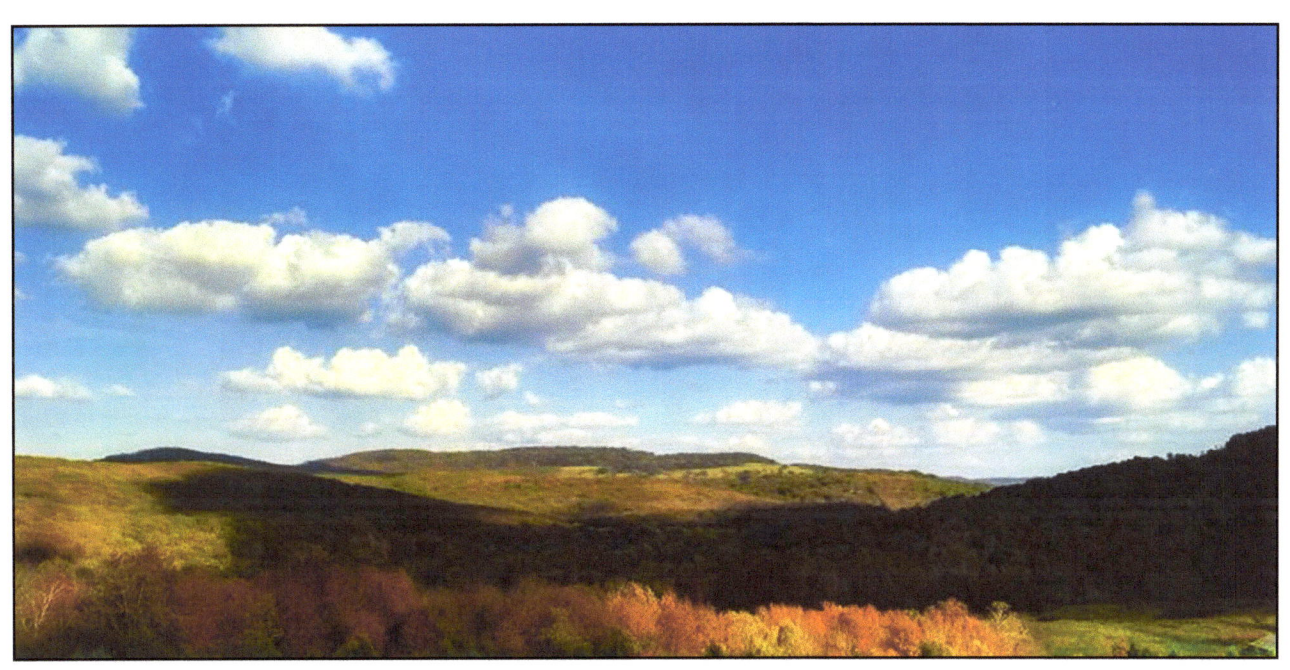

The Ozarks, Arkansas

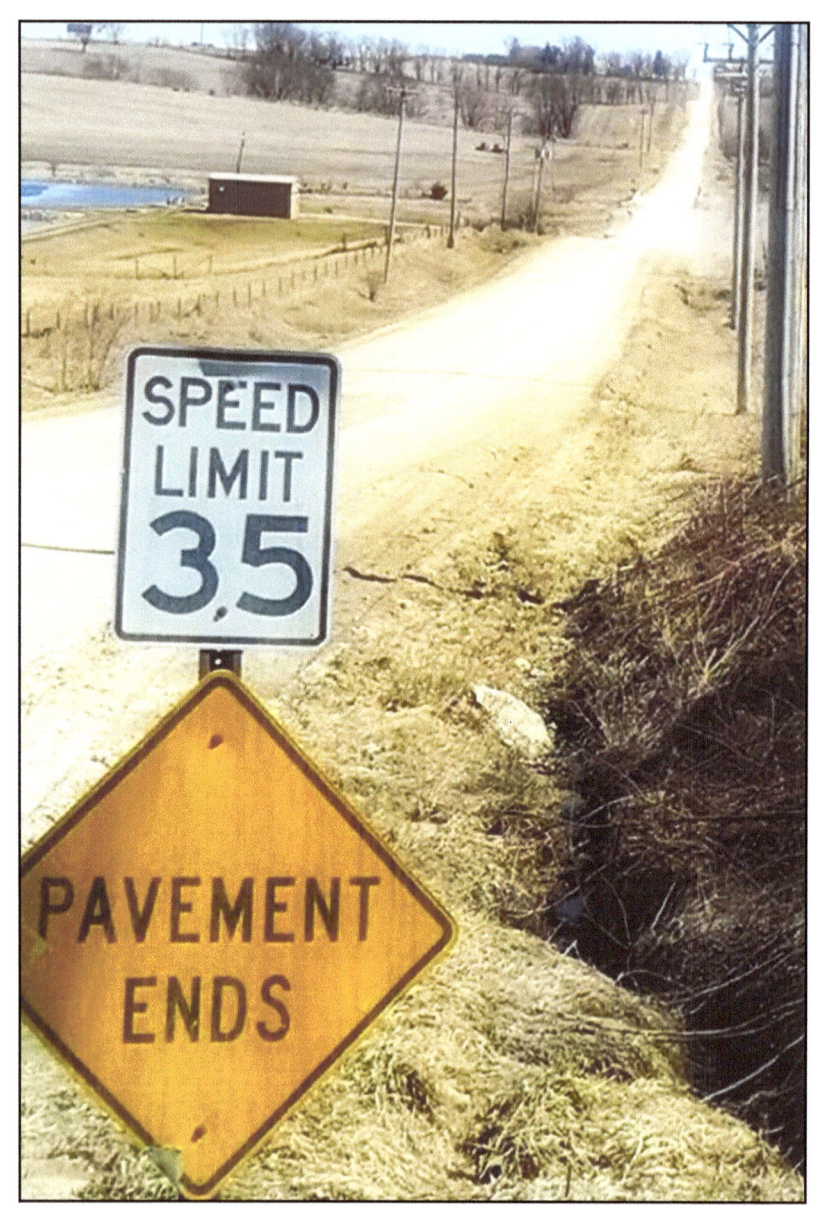

And the road goes on....Napoleon, Ohio